AN ALCOVE IN THE HEART
WW II Letters of Sidney Diamond to Estelle Spero

Edited by Estelle Spero Lynch

The past is never dead. It's not even past.
—Wm. Faulkner

What thou lovest well remains....
—Ezra Pound

New Jewel Services Inc.
www.NJSInc.com

www.AlcoveInTheHeart.com

First edition published by AuthorHouse 2004

Second edition published by New Jewel Services Inc. 2011

ISBN: 9780615472638 (0-615-47263-X)

Printed in the United States of America

This book is printed on acid-free paper.

Read more about the book, with updates, at http://AlcoveInTheHeart.com

ACKNOWLEDGEMENTS

I want to express my heartfelt thanks to Andrew Carroll, editor of *War Letters*, for recognizing the extraordinary qualities of Sidney Diamond's letters, as well as of the young man who wrote them, and for encouraging me in pursuing their publication.

My husband, Louis, has been patient as I sat before the computer, and has consistently offered me the support and understanding without which I could not have completed this book.

Jack Butler, Lt. Col., US Army (Ret.), and the late Harold House, platoon leaders in the the battle for Luzon, as was Sidney Diamond, were most helpful in answering my questions about that battle. Jack is preparing a book on the history of the 82nd Chemical Mortar Battalion.

Contents

viii

PREFACE

More than sixty years have passed since Sidney Diamond wrote the letters in this book. Yet, in reading them again, I once again hear his voice—his seriousness when discussing his deepest beliefs, his chuckling when he was about to say something humorous, his tenderness and passion when expressing his love.

These are letters of war and love. He spared me descriptions of the most horrific aspects of the battles in which he fought; he was able, when given half a chance, to find humor to attempt to provide emotional relief for both of us, each of us concerned about the welfare of the other.

Most of Sid's letters were very long and covered several subjects. It was difficult to choose letters from among the 525 I kept all these years, all of which seem memorable to me. Where the letters were too long to include in their entirety, I have chosen what I think are the most interesting portions, indicating with ellipses where parts have been omitted. Otherwise, the letters stand as they were written, with only the addition of words or parts of words that were omitted shown in brackets, dates not actually given on the letters but readily inferred from the sequence of events, shown in parentheses, and a question mark in brackets when I could not decipher a word.

When Sid was sent overseas, he was no longer able to save my letters, so that few of mine survive, but some of these are included, when they seem necessary to explain what was happening between us at a particular time.

Sid's letters convey a picture of his need and determination to maintain the closeness which had characterized our relationship before he enlisted. In these letters, written often at white heat under trying circumstances, his "voice" comes through loud and clear.

INTRODUCTION

In the summer of 1939 I began a correspondence with a young man named Sidney Diamond, a correspondence that was to last, under various circumstances, for a number of years.

We had met in August 1938 in Mullaly Park, which adjoined Macombs Dam Park in the Bronx, near the Yankee Stadium. Although it was already clear to the people of Europe and to many Americans that war was inevitable, even imminent, I had just turned fourteen in June. My small world of friends, school, expanding interests in music, art, and literature, included the threat of world events only peripherally.

Mullaly was, in essence, a very large playground and playing field and included a large brick building which today we would call a community center. Outdoors boys played softball or basketball, girls and boys played a version of platform tennis, indoors there were ping-pong tables, badminton courts, and tables with game boards. Across the street were handball and tennis courts. It was a small complete world for adolescents.

Sid and I knew all the boys and the few girls who made Mullaly their summer base. Yet very soon after we met, it was Sid and I who became inseparable friends. I don't know just how this came about. He was sixteen, nice-looking, but not yet especially handsome, well-built, giving an impression of strength held in reserve. He had strong features, with very deep-set eyes. I recognized in him, at first at an instinctive level, what I could later name as integrity, reliability, kindness, and modesty. What used to be called "character." And intelligence. And all leavened with humor.

Sid and I became pals, meeting at my house or at Mullaly, participating in all the activities of Mullaly and walking all over the neighborhoods of the Bronx. At the end of the day he would walk me home, which was an apartment house on Shakespeare Avenue, near Jerome Avenue, and then continue on to Nelson Avenue, where he lived. He told me years later, reminiscing, that the second time he walked me home he said to himself, "I want to marry that girl."

From the beginning I saw that he was someone special, to whom I could trust large and small concerns, doubts, and hopes. He felt the same trust in me.

"I like you," he would write to me later, "—everything about you—the stray hair over the forehead, the nose, the ears—the neck— the body—the knees—take it back on the knees—they hurt when you kick—the feet—the blisters you get so I have to make believe I'm helping you walk—I like your conversation—more for the times you don't make sense than when you do—I like the way you're—well— cute—I like you when you're serious—nothing about you displeases me—I like your firmness of opinion—Darn it all—You're a big business—but no liabilities—I love you—"

And a month later he writes: "You're the one I'm thinking of—The you that is so soft and warm—so pleasant—gentle—kind—You that is the unsophisticated—Lacking of airs and superficialities--...The you that arouses calm thought, complacent happiness, violent passion— The you that I embrace in my dreams—"

It still warms my heart to feel these words.

We shared interests. Both of us were serious about our studies, enjoyed reading, going to museums (then free), taking advantage of all the low-cost cultural opportunities available in New York City.

In the fall of 1938, Sid entered the senior year at Stuyvesant High School, a school for intellectually gifted boys, and I became a senior at Walton High School. We saw each other often, and the bond between us grew. The following year he entered City College to study chemical engineering, and I was accepted at Hunter College, to major in speech and English. Having been a Boy Scout and then an Assistant Scout Master for several years, he joined Alpha Phi Omega, the service fraternity at City College. We spent many happy evenings at the fraternity house, dancing, socializing, and, when everyone else had left, entwined in each other's arms in the inner room, listening to records.

We were welcome in each other's homes. His parents were Russian Jews, his mother a charming, heavy-set woman with a love of opera and fine literature which she was unable to express at this time in her life. She and her husband sold dresses from their apartment. What would have been the living room held the racks of dresses, and Sid's room, until 4 p.m. each day, was the dressing room. His parents' room was the stockroom. I seldom had the opportunity or occasion to speak to his father, who acted as buyer for the store, but I could feel the love between Sid and his parents.

My father was an optometrist, my mother, an elementary school teacher. While Sid's family suffered greatly during the Depression, I was not aware of any hardship in mine. But my paternal and maternal grandparents had been immigrants, so Sid's parents were well within my experience and affection.

Mullaly occasionally had dances to recorded music in the community building. During one of these dances, in 1939, the song Love Walked In was played, and I felt a strange new sensation, which I was not yet ready to call love. I never, then or later, mentioned this epiphany to Sid. It was that same year, in late June, that we went to Steeplechase Park in Coney Island, which was a very popular amusement park in those days. We went on one of the tamer rides, called The Caterpillar, because the seats, which rotated around a sinuous track, were covered with green gauze. At the end of the ride, after asking whether it would be all right, Sid kissed me for the first time. He said long afterward, humorously explaining his having asked permission, "I knew I loved you, and I didn't want to maul you."

That summer and the following one, with Sid working as a waiter at a children's camp, we wrote each other often, but I was busy with many friends, girls and boys. While I knew that he was "special" to me, we had not yet exchanged professions of love. His letters show the restraint of a boy who didn't know whether his love was returned. Most of them relate what one would expect from a young waiter at a children's camp—hiking into town, meeting girls, "battles" with canoes in the middle of the lake, getting along with the bosses, putting on shows for the adjacent adult camp. He studied fencing and boxing with two of the counselors, he worked on his ballroom dancing, he was the one anyone who was sick or in need of time off would turn to.

In one letter written in 1940 he wrote about one of the other waiters, with his typical concern for the feelings and well-being of others: "He's very young and acts even younger. When I first met up with him I was of the opinion that he was a horrible dullard. The fact is the majority of the people here think the same way. Upon investigation I've discovered that he is slightly deaf. This handicap makes him do and say things which, of course, are utterly stupid. I've tried to educate the other boys to this inability to hear that hinders Eugene but they insist upon mocking and deriding him."

Feeling for me is expressed shyly: "It's starting to rain—I guess I can prolong this letter for a short while since there's that damned hateful rain to imprison me. Frankly, if I've got to be shut up there's nothing I can think of that would be more pleasant than writing to and thinking of you.—Very glib if I say so myself—There I go again taking back things I meant in the first place only didn't like the way I said it—again—oh well!!"

Occasionally a serious concern surfaces. "As far as school is concerned," he writes in 1939, "I feel extremely anxious to get back into harness again, but somehow I've got a strange feeling of anxiety about the future I can't explain but it's there."

It was on September 1, 1939 that Hitler marched into Poland.

In another letter of that summer, Sid wrote of a veteran of World War I who worked at the camp: "His generation has not profited at all from the lessons of the last war. Instead they seem to be desirous of making their sons and daughters undergo a worse holocaust. They seem to think that this generation is too happy….It all seems so…God damned hypocritical."

Despite his foreboding about the future, in which he was all too prescient, the fun and fellowship of being a waiter in a children's camp continued. By the summer of 1941 our feelings for each other had been expressed, and he felt able to write: "Last night—lying silently—stars overhead—girl sound asleep beside me—victrola crackling—Cesar Frank's Symphony in D minor—There it was—atmosphere, mood, music—Where, oh where were you??? 'Stelle it wasn't fair—I was lonely—lonely for you!"

And again: " 'Stelle, dearest, all the damned activity in the world—all the girls in the camp, all the fun that can happen doesn't take away for a moment the ever-present—ever-satisfying,—ever pleasant thoughts of you—Gosh but I miss you—What's the use of dancing, dating, prancing—if it only makes me more lonely for you. Nuts!—"

Our love for each other had grown to the point where it was the most important part of our existence. Sid felt for a very long time that he was unworthy of my love and was sure that it couldn't be real. One night he said, as if to a third person, "I make her laugh, I entertain her, and so she goes out with me." It was certainly true that we laughed a good deal together. Either one of us—usually he—could start the "entertainment," and the other would continue until we would be laughing joyously wherever we were, even waiting for the train at the 167th Street station in the Bronx.

In the fall of 1941 sure of my love for Sid and of his for me, feeling that all was right in the best of all possible worlds, that nothing could intrude on our commitment to each other, I walked down the long, slightly downhill street leading from the Grand Concourse down 167 Street to Jerome Avenue, telling myself, "This is the happiest time of your life, and you're never going to forget it."

Sid and 'Stelle May 1941

On December 7, 1941, we were catapulted into war and out of our dreams of the future by the Japanese attack on Pearl Harbor.

As soon as we heard of the attack, Sid wanted to enlist. His friends and fraternity brothers, he said, seemed to be looking for ways to avoid being drafted— "Don't they want to win this thing?"

And so the first rift between us opened. Finishing his course of study, to qualify for an assignment in the armed forces commensurate with his education and abilities, seemed to me a sensible and honorable choice. His sense of duty conflicted with his love for me and his desire to spare his parents anxiety. For four months my entreaties postponed his enlisting.

On April 24, 1942, he entered Fort Dix as a private, a raw recruit, and a new kind of correspondence between us began.

Sid's letters of the almost three years following his enlistment portray the evolution of an idealistic boy into a first-rate soldier, who came to experience the horror, exhaustion, and deep conviction of the human waste of war. The rigors of training, and, at first, the joy of encountering people of very different backgrounds, the experiences associated with new places and new responsibilities—all find expression in his wonderful letters— along with the humor which was part of his nature. And the overwhelming love which he felt for me.

I kept all of Sid's letters, tied into little packets arranged by date. When I moved, they moved with me, along with a few of my letters and some of my diaries. The humanity, wit, and intelligence of his letters show an extraordinary young man whom I loved and still love.

Sixty-six years have passed since we met in Mullaly Park. He deserves to live on.

It is my hope that through his letters his spirit and the richness of his mind and heart will shine and endure.

PART 1: 1942

AN ALCOVE IN THE HEART

In the summer of 1939, Sidney Diamond, then seventeen years old, was a waiter at a children's camp in the Catskill Mountains. We had been good friends since the previous year, and we carried on a lively correspondence while he was away. In one of his letters, he wrote, "As far as school is concerned, I feel extremely anxious to get back into harness again, but somehow I've got a strange feeling of anxiety about the future I can't explain but it's there."

Hitler invaded Poland on September 1, 1939, and two days later war against the Axis (Germany and Italy) was declared by France and Britain.

In the United States, emotion ran high, with programs designed to raise patriotic fervor. I found the blatant appeal to emotion distasteful, but Sid wrote from camp in 1940, "... let us look at this matter from a different point of view. It becomes absolutely essential to bring the youth of the country around to the idea that patriotism and nationalism are not a farce but a necessary factor in the well-being of a nation in a world disinclined towards international friendliness...I'm sorry, I like my freedom and I see no reason in shirking from the task of preserving it."

Later, he would add, reporting on heated discussions among the staff at camp engendered by differing points of view on what the role of the United States should be, "I firmly believe that to fight hell you've got to acclimate yourselves to the devil's tactics."

In the Pacific, relations between Japan and the United States had been deteriorating for some time. Early on December 7, 1941, Japan bombed Pearl Harbor, on the Hawaiian island of Oahu, while negotiations with Washington were supposedly being pursued. On December 8 the United States and Great Britain, also under attack in the Pacific, declared war on Japan.

Loving Sid as I did, and knowing his deep respect for the ideals for which his country stood, I should not have been stunned and devastated by his telling me that he wanted to enlist. But I was. How could he want to leave me, just when we two were so sure of our love for each other? The next few months were filled with my tears and his impassioned explanations. Since he was ten years old, he maintained, he had always said that if we got into a war, he'd be the first to go. He quoted what I did not then recognize as from a poem by A. E. Housman: "I shall have lived a little while/Before I die forever." That he could think this way sent a chill down my spine. I couldn't understand his eagerness to go. As an outstanding student of science in high school, now nearing the end of his third year of study in chemical engineering at City College, why could he not finish his degree? College students in the sciences were not being drafted. Once he finished and was drafted, he could enter whichever branch of service he chose. Or he could get a defense job.

There were times when he seemed to want to retract his decision to enlist. My arguments achieved a delay of a few months but were ultimately unsuccessful. His parents, his friends, even the mentor who had imbued him with fierce love of country—all tried to persuade him not to act hastily.

Shortly before leaving for Fort Dix

But in the middle of April, he left for the Fort Dix Reception Center as a raw recruit. I was heartbroken, unable to picture life without Sid for the years of what I felt would be a long war. My friend Natalie's mother remarked lightly, "Don't worry, Estelle. Only the good die young." To which I replied, "That's just what I'm afraid of."

I visited Sid at Fort Dix on May 3, and he wrote to me the following day.

Co. B 1229-R.C.
Fort Dix, N.J.
Bun!

Since last we met, (ah platitudes!) much water has poured violently beneath the not too steady bridge! —— yes, Estelle, the inevitable has happened, don't scold — I lost my temper!!! ——got into a combat with fists. —These fisticuffs (if we might call them such) started suddenly, lasted a few moments — and were broken up when the party got rough! — Here are all the lurid details — I'll attempt to be as rational and unprejudiced as is possible. —

1. There exists a clique of three or four gentlemen who feel it their responsibility to uphold the morale of the men by continually harassing the men with childish pranks such as half sheeting beds, smearing cold cream and shoe polish on unsuspecting slumberers, forcibly shaving some.

2. All these a certain "guy" endured, realizing that it's to be expected during the first few days. As the days grew into a week and still the nuisances continued, this same guy said — "enough!"

3. Mind you, this "guy" approached this thing in a coldly scientific manner. He reasoned as follows a) These men would continue unless stopped b) not only would they molest newcomers but would enjoy bothering "veterans" — taking advantage of friendships acquired c) They had never been subjected to the same treatment d) and most important they did not realize what it was to be humbled.

4. Well — "guy" was comfortable loafing in bed, — attempting to read — suffering slightly from an overdose of cookies, a heavy dinner and an innoculation received in the afternoon when suddenly he found himself flying through the air, bed and all following him — When he landed bed and all fell down on top of big guy!!

Well, why continue — verbal argument was useless — so now they don't bother "guy" anymore and people think "guy" used to play football!!…

…At present I'm seated at the same bench we occupied Sunday. The band is playing "As the Caissons Go Rolling…"…

…Darling, I have no regrets, no longings, no homesickness except the gnawing hunger to be near you—to speak with you—to press your hand in mine and stroll…

'Stelle, I shall attempt, at least, to argue your thoughts of the unworthiness of the effort I am, through my own choosing, engaging in.

Our mutual friend Thomas Paine has aptly said "My country is the world and my religion is to do good!" Let's ponder over this for a moment.

5

It's true as Goethe suggests that in peace time every one concerns himself with sweeping his own doorstep and minding his own business and things will go well; but, at present the world (which we recognize as our country) fights hopelessly in a maelstrom as it is gradually and seemingly inevitably sucked into chaos...'Stelle—our country is the entire world and mankind our countrymen!

Whew-what brought that on—cool off Sid—take a shower!!...

Oh well—hm-hm-hm, I hear your mother whistling—Good night sweetheart— Love—

Yours—always!

Sid

An amateur graphologist at the camp analyzed Sid's character from his handwriting and, amazingly, recognized his firmness in beliefs and loyalties, modesty, and persistence. Yes, this was the Sid I knew.

On May 10 Sid was sent to Edgewood Arsenal to join the Chemical Warfare Service, a new Army service where he felt his education in chemical engineering would be especially useful.

Hello sweet —

...Can't express my elation and satisfaction with the new post... Everyone makes it a point of behaving like a gentleman and soldier. Persons here are proud of the service they're in — The Chemical Warfare Service is a comparatively new branch of the army — corporal informs us that it's merely a year and a half old. It acts its age — young, vibrant, enthusiastic, courageous, and, above all, eager!

When we arrived I was "overcome" by the odor along the road — resembled very much the Qualitative Analysis Lab — Very very nostalgic! Immediately upon arrival they issued gas masks — It seems they (gas masks) are to become as much a part of our equipment and personalities as a pair of underdraws!! — The barracks are far superior to those at camp (Fort) Dix — more showers, wash basins etc.—less crowded — officers and personnel zealous and chummy! I'm certain I'm going to enjoy my "sojourn" here. As for visits and trips home — During the first five weeks it will be absolutely impossible for me to get a pass. Also, going A.W.O.L. is punished severely. —After the five weeks, passes are issued for weekends — about once every two weeks. — At the termination of the five weeks we attend school and more training—for nine weeks more!...From that point — well — again —your guess is as good as mine — Men from this

6

service are assigned to either the infantry, field artillery, motorized [?], air corps — about any place except, possibly, the coast artillery. Then — more training! Frankly — I like it! —

Since I last spoke to you I've — gone to a movie; dissipated to death on ice cream and cocoa cola; ate spaghetti, gabbed an entire evening; traveled about 170 miles; read a Time; changed from winter woolens to summer cottons; fell in love all over again with — —you; worried myself half sick about where I'd end up; thought of you! — almost died when they emptied the rest of the train at Aberdeen Ordinance Training Center…Fell asleep on train — dreamt of you! — That's about all —…

I cannot express adequately how gratified I am at being here — as soon as I can leave camp I'll be home — It's just about a four hour trip by train —

Here's a bit of irony for you — after receiving two punishment details at Fort Dix's kitchens I'm to be "present, dressed for work, at the company kitchen, tomorrow morning"! I don't mind though — By the way, at this place we don't stand on line and have food thrown into tin trays. We are served on tables with real honest-to-goodness dishes and silverware — no benches — individual seats — classy!…

> I love you
> Your
> Sid

Sid had said he did not want to end up as a lab technician. I asked, "Why not?"

Edgewood Arsenal
Maryland
Good afternoon bun——

This is the second letter today—Reason? Well, first because I want to be as close to you as possible –and—writing is very near making a one-sided conversation (at last!) — Second, because your last letter asked a great many questions — very blunt, direct, and scathing questions — you ask for explanations — you require definite answers— okay—

Do I want you? — emphatically yes!!

Will I do my duty cheerfully — I always have !

How can I say that you are the most important thing in my life and in the next breath say I'd not be happy if the tiny bit of hope we (and it is we!) have, was protected by Uncle Sam? ——Fact to consider — an entire Laboratory company of the C.W.S. was destroyed (400 men) at

Pearl Harbor — a man can "get it" any where, any time, and in any branch of the service.

I know full well all I've given up to follow my conscience ——— take my conscience away from me, take away my ability to think strongly and steadfastly — take that away and, well you could have the empty hulk at bargain prices! — I mean that seriously — You'd never have to worry — you'd always have your fellow. But remember just as well as you could control him and influence him so could others — He'd never belong to you and you alone —

Fact to consider — I understand that my company will be made into a maintenance and pregnating unit — non-combatant. They will, however, probably be somewhere near the troops — — just as good as weather observer or forecaster. —

Cont'd at 9:30 P.M.

'Stelle this is probably the one and only time you'll get me in this mood but I just want you to take a few facts into consideration when you feel blue or angry at me for what I've done —

I've got no right to complain — sick, tired, half dead or worked to tears, there's none whom I could write or speak to in order to ease the suffering — my parents would suffer with me — my alleged pals would smile and remark "Well – he asked for it!" — you, perhaps a little sympathy – perhaps you may feel the way my parents would — hence I can't go grousing to you. For each hurt — both physical and mental that I've got to squelch within me there grows a callous – a hardening of mind — a hardening of thoughts — Its good! Very good ——— I'll learn to be good and selfish — I'll hoard all my pains — I'll be happy. My only pals are my buddies — as the sergeant puts it — "The man that'll give you a slug o' water when your guts are hangin' out!" — Just remember I'm human like you – capable of sensing fear, anxiety, wrong ——— I know now who the real people are! —

I could be enduring the worst tortures and yet have no kind opening to pour my heart out.— Yep — I understand a lot more about the so called "hard" boys — Take it from me they're not happy — They're like me — stubborn in ideals — stubborn in what they think is right — They've learned what I'm trying to understand.

Oh, let's cut this out — please forgive me — a man's got to 'blow his top" occasionally — good for the soul or something—

You can tear this up or burn it or save it as a psychological study of the fox battling the dogs nibbling at his toes.— He bites because he's exhausted — all his physical and mental cunning couldn't keep the dogs from biting – as a last resort — back to the wall – he bites— viciously!!!

I realize this is sort of morbid stuff – but that's the way I feel —

You're my pal. 'Stelle, if I thought this goo was being taken the way the rest of them have received it, I'd shut up as tight as a clam— you know me — Now I see the advantages of giving a man a nickel for a bowl of soup—You're comrades for a moment and then both of you can walk away free!! No hurts,—no talks—no misunderstanding.

Ha — I just recalled that evening you gushed out your anger at some play director – give me the same consideration I gave you — don't sympathize just say – okay Sid — we're still "guy and girl" — let it pour and then go out and have a good time — okay????—

Peculiar how a guy can lose his sense of equilibrium over this nonsense.

I'd better close – no – not that I want to leave you – I'd rather sleep on it and try and forget it.

I love you – always – your
Sid

I tried to assuage Sid's disappointment at the lack of support he felt, and to assure him of mine.

May 19, 1942
Sweetheart,

I just finished reading your second Saturday letter, and it seemed to deserve an immediate answer.

Fella, I'm not sure I quite understood everything. I gather that your friends have been getting you down. Have I been very bad, darling?

You see, I tried not to be scolding or "I told you so." Really and truly, now that everything can be looked at more objectively I know with my heart and soul, as well as my brain, that you had to do what you thought right. Please – understand that. And if ever my letters are "grousey" or scolding, it's just because I'm alone, at night, when I want terribly to be with you, and in those moments my heart rules my head. See?

Sid – more than anything else in the world, I'd like you to think I understand you a little, and to know that, no matter what you do, it's o.k. by me. If you do it, your motive is right, whether or not your reasoning is.

Don't, don't, don't become hard and selfish; it won't make you happy. If you're lonely, you can say so without my saying "I told you so." If you're tired, sick, weary, don't "hoard your pains." Don't get that callous, sweet. Can't you see that that's the worst thing that could happen?

You know, from your letter, I can't tell whether I'm included in your anger, too - I guess not – except that you list as advantages of giving a man a bowl of soup "no hurts no talks no misunderstandings," and that sounds like me.

Please don't try to explain. I know you have to be in the mood for this sort of thing.

I want to be your pal, Sid — the kind you can tell things to without being "reproached," without fearing a "smirk." Remember? Only don't grow callous.

You're the person I want to stick by and confide in for all time, till that adolescent day after forever. It would be a terrible thing if we lost the "rapport" which has made us so close —

The radio is playing a jazz song, and the last line of one of the stanzas was, "you're my necessity, I'd be lost without you."

That's the way it is, fella. So don't lose anything in you which makes you as wonderful as you are – even what you consider your weaknesses.

As far as your friends are concerned, don't be angry at them because they don't understand (sounds like Bernie). Either they haven't your vision, your ideals, or they love you as I do, and are afraid for you, as I sometimes am – (more than sometimes). Don't blame them; they are just certain that you, because of what you are, have the stuff in you that the world will need in peace time just as much (I think more) than in war time.

Yours – first, last, always,

Estelle

In his next letter, Sid apologized for his outburst, explaining that he had had "a horribly annoying sore throat...an excruciating headache, a consistent and ceaseless cough..." He also assured me, "If I feel angry with anyone it could never include you."

My life at Hunter College, which I had entered in the fall of 1939 at the age of fifteen, continued. I was taking courses, among others, in speech correction, with Dr. Egbert Spadino, and courses in theater.

May 24, 1942

Sweetheart! How I love you. Even when you get me into embarrassing situations. To explain - Spadino raced down the steps after me the other day bellowing my name.

"Didn't you lose something, Miss Spero?"

10

"No, not I."

"Oh, yes, you did."

And so on. Finally –

"A letter to Sid, wasn't it?"

Well, I must have turned purple. You don't know about those letters I don't mail — I write them either when I'm terribly blue or awfully affectionate, or just plain chatty — and I pray that this letter was chatty and nothing more! Spadino, the dog, would have no scruples about reading it — although he swears he didn't. Death, where is thy sting?

Last night this play producer was in school from 5–11:15 ringing bells and rigging scenery for the dress rehearsal of a play one of Harvey's classes is giving. The play is Cradle Song, a faintly rancid affair about nuns in a convent. Yours truly sat backstage and rang bells better than bells have ever been rung in the history of the theatre. This was all done with a five-foot, heavy, musically-inclined piece of pipe. This versatile instrument was a door, a clock, and chapel bells. Everything was fine until my hand slipped once, and instead of hitting the thing with the felt part of the stick, the wood struck the pipe, and sounded like a four-alarm fire. Oh, well.

> Have to go now. Sleep tight.
>
> Estelle

Later that same day, I wrote again, wondering what Sid's reaction would be to the news I had just received about my friend Natalie, my best friend at the time.

Sid darling—

Oh, hon – I'm so excited I can hardly hold the pen – Nat just called. She's getting married June 28 – not to Gene, but to Bert, whom she knows for a month and a half. The last time I saw her she had gone out with him four times. Isn't that wonderful, sweet? I'm going to be a bridesmaid. It's going to be held at the Jewish Portuguese synagogue on 70th something Street, and it has to be a secret, because she'll get kicked out of school if they find out. Bert is a dental student, and he's got his commission and will be leaving for the army when the term's over.

Oh hon – you can't imagine how my heart is pounding. I could just bawl, mostly through joy, and a teeny weeny bit of envy, and a tremendous desire that she get the swellest guy in the world, next to you, and wonder that she has the courage and spunk. Do you think I'll catch her flowers? Sid – I'm going to tell you what's been going on in my imitation of a mind, and if you like, you can call it the hysteria of the moment. I've been

11

wishing that we had the courage to do what Nat's doing, and I've been wishing that for the past two weeks, mostly. Tell me if you think I'm crazy; I know you must. Darling, tell me what you think…

Isn't it wonderful, though! Nat, the little innocent I had to educate getting married June 28 – and not to Gene. Lordy!

That's all I wanted to tell you right now. That, and also that you mean more to me than anything in the world. I love you, always,

Estelle

Sid's reply was written at 10 p.m. the evening of the day he received my letter.

Dear sweet 'Stelle-

It's late, terribly late but I've got to get this off. — This has been gnawing my insides out all day- (this A.M. received your letter dealing with Natalie's great happiness!) —…

Please please forgive anything that might sound unkind — I'm in a hurry — I can't bother calculating exactly how you'll interpret what I have to say!!!!

Let's look at this matter objectively — Here's a fellow, myself, desperately in love with a girl—yourself.——He's in the army —— His life is a gamble–a great gamble — He loves the girl so much he occasionally thinks of giving her a brush off so that she'd go after someone a little more stable in his position in the present and the future. Unfortunately his love has turned him a bit selfish and he thinks, perhaps, that she too might take that gamble —

This soldier fully realizes that this young lady could also meet a fellow, know him for a few months and then go off and get married. He is aware that it would probably be most advantageous to her —— He looks at a score sheet totaling his assets???

1. He can't guarantee physical presence
2. He can't promote financial stability
3. Hasn't reached his majority
4. Can't see a future after the War for Survival
5. Can offer nothing but love & devotion which may or may not be enough.
6. Well you know — Blah Blah and so on.

Now look, I'm approaching you as one intelligent "soldier" to another. You look over the map — understand the lay of the land — pick your own route, 'Stelle, you <u>are</u> the boss. Realize, that, as far as courage to consummate our love is concerned, I have no fears. I'm certain of my affection for you. I simply want <u>you</u> to think it over and decide which is the best course of action for <u>you.</u>

'Stelle, I've already proposed —I'll leave the rest up to you — Whatever you decide is best as far as <u>your</u> happiness is concerned will be my goal. — engagement, marriage, continued friendship, breaking up — anything <u>you</u> wish ——

Look — the preliminary training period has been cut from 13 weeks to 8 weeks — after that probably some school or perhaps transfer!!...

I'm going to hit the hay — Back to the room — and the solitude of the mosquito net!!

Yours —
Sid

I found Sid's reply upsetting, and wrote to tell him so.

Received your "reply" this morning. I won't attempt to answer it, except to say that this is one time I won't even try to make a decision. And, my oh-so-wonderfully-unselfish lover, henceforth you will have to take any initiative that will be taken — friendship, marriage, or even breaking-up — if you feel that unselfish.

You see, I have a tendency to think that maybe, when you went, you were not consciously and deliberately sacrificing me to your nobility, and this tendency makes me think and do very strange things.

Thoughts of love could cause absent-mindedness at highly inappropriate times, as Sid indicated in the following letter. The "bear rug" referred to was one of the items of furnishings we had talked about having in our future living quarters.

I love you so much that it isn't funny any longer. After I'd completed the call this evening I walked...dreamily along thinking about a bear rug when there before me were two officers (gold leaves on their shoulders) — Proper courtesy demanded that I salute — What did I do?? — stared hard and long at their faces, glanced at the leaves (major and lieutenant colonel) and calmly walked by!!! — When I'd gone five paces past them I stopped! — realized my mistake — half turned about — half saluted — just sort of

13

hesitated between saluting and going forward! — At that point I realized the stupidity of deliberately turning about — and walked on! — much to the amusement of officers and gang of enlisted men near by!!...

We've been changed now to a chemical weapons co. which means this — instead of going anywhere as a unit we'll probably be shipped out to the different branches of the service — infantry, field artillery, etc. I pray not to be assigned to "pebble dusting" (infantry) — But — well — as you say — "I asked for it!"...

Closing now.
Your
Sid

Peter Ibbetson was a popular play or movie in which separated lovers meet by appointment in their dreams. We had set June 4, the date of the following letter, as our Peter Ibbetson night.

June 4, 1942
Good evening, sweetheart —

I love you ——Fine way to open a letter — yes — Fine way!!! — I love you!!!

I'm going to attempt to write as much as humanly possible in this limited space of time and the constant noise and bustle of the gang in the day room. At present — Bonnie Baker's bawling through "Oh Johnny" — Somebody's elbow's running back and forth before my right eye — He's winding victrola — another Bonnie record—I object!!!

Got to shine shoes, pretty up clothes for tomorrow's inspection — get the back of my head shaved! — etc.—Get some sleep — Tomorrow we go to firing range!!! —

Oh about that selection from the New Yorker — It's from a short story entitled "The Magic Hour!" — quotation usted — "No man who's away from home nights can expect faithfulness from a woman if she's worth anything!!" — Then you question in red pencil — "Am I faithful or worth something?"

Occasionally, sweet, you can ask the darnedest questions!!! One could delve deeply into the philosophy of love and its entanglements, I guess. Here's the plain and simple truth —— I love you dearly, selfishly, —I care little for anyone else ——The hours of unhappiness and loneliness are brightened some by the knowledge that my pal's still my pal! You have no worries as far as my continued affection is concerned. What I ask of you is the simple courtesy of letting me know when you're finished with our love

— I only ask that you save me the humiliation of realizing my words of unbounding devotion are falling upon deaf or perhaps amused ears ——

Deep down, underneath, there's a burning desire to say, be true to me!! ——love me as I love you!! Never stop loving me!!! ——Think of me!!!——I want you always, I don't care to share you with anyone — Bonnie Baker's now doing "Pinch me!" — appropriate, what!!! Aw – What the devil!!!

Have you met mosquitoes the size of horse flies — with the cunning of a tiger; the ferocity of a wounded lion; the speed of a dive bomber— the Maryland mosquito strafes the CWS men. — They're astounding! You probably wouldn't believe me when I tell you I could hear one of them sawing through my net last night — You're right — I wouldn't believe it either — But they're the darnedest, most aggressive fresh little imps you'll ever encounter!!! —

Today — as I mentioned we went on that ten-mile hike — full pack etc. — When a commanding officer deliberately walks his company a mile off the road so that it may be able to crawl through a squashy, sloshy disgusting mud area — oh well!

…This A.M. we had slides on chemical warfare protective measures, decontamination, gas proof shelters, etc. nothing outstanding. You can see that I'm rushing this now — must go — I'll meet you tonight — pray I'm not too tired to dream of you — I don't need morpheus and a cot to make me think of you —— Any time of day or night is a proper occasion…

> I love you
> Your
> Sid

I replied, "When I fall out of this hypnoidal state called love, I'll tell you — don't worry about that. I'll never have to."

The description of the rigors of training made very clear to me that we were living in two separate worlds, joined only by love.

(Lew Ayres was a movie actor who became a conscientious objector.)

(June 7)
Hello darling —

Excuse pencil, haste, incoherency — It's now 8:45 — 9.00 lights go out in barracks and we've got to clean rifles — I've been out on the rifle range from 6 A.M. to 8 P.M. — we were up at 3:45 in order to get set at range. — Laid mile of wire for telephone from range to cross road — fired 30 rounds — man before me was a typical Sergeant York — me??? — well

— on the slow fire –pretty good –on the rapid fire (ten shots, 60 seconds) — well I made a lot of noise, anyway, from twelve until 8 I was in the target pit — hoisting targets up and down, — marking hits and signaling scores. — a shell ricocheted off the edge of the target against the cement wall and finally fell (gently) on my shoulder. — I'm saving it — In the hope that I can tell my — perhaps, our grandchildren that it was the nearest a bullet ever came to me!! —

We ate two meals in the field — became very dirty!!! — Fine way to spend a Sunday, that's all I can say!! — ...

...I didn't mention our date Friday night in yesterday's letter...they tell me I shouted "Don't do it" in my sleep!...You came to me time and time again. Nothing much except just your face— you kept scowling at me. Once or twice you smiled — occasionally you'd appear walking with me — Sometimes I'd tie you up with somebody else (must be when I shouted "don't do it!") Ah, worry, — ah — love!

Concerning Zeke and the job — 'Stelle a lot of illusions I've had about people, about rationalization, about objective outlook have been worked out of me. — I have this to say at present! — If he believes strongly that this war is a false one, that some of the issues involved don't concern him, if he is definitely of the opinion that his participation in the war would run entirely against his nature — I'd admire him more, if he'd have the strength of his opinion to either attempt to get into a conscientious objector's camp or even spend the war period in jail ——A man can't talk strongly of opinions and beliefs and then, when the test comes, begin to look for "outs."

I've met too many men who are undergoing hell; an environment, and work entirely alien to their upbringing — Being cursed, worked, scolded, punished —— Men with 2B, 3A, etc. classifications.

Men with 1A — — They don't squawk!!——Men cry about their wives but never about fighting or about dying. — I sincerely respect Lew Ayres for his strength of mind and character — —for his willingness to sacrifice life, career, friends because of a firmness of thought. Zeke can do as he pleases ...but I'd say Zeke ought to make up his mind — definitely, irrevocably about how he feels and act accordingly!!! — — again — oh well !!! — its none of my affair and he'd probably say so!...

I love you, sweetheart —...

Just heard that we'll definitely be on the range next Sunday...

We've been going now for 7 days without a stop. There's another 13 ahead. — No Sunday, no rest — Just work — —

Spent the time in the pit listening to the bullets. —— I became expert enough (towards the end) to distinguish when my target was being shot at, by the noise the gun and bullet made. — The most fascinating sound I've yet to encounter is that of a ricocheting shell — — a sort of ping!! (draw it out) God, those rifles make an awful racket. When I walked up to the fire line I was scared half out of my shirtsleeves at the first shot. After awhile, however, I'd just wink my eyes at the blast. —— Frankly, I was afraid of the damn things — ...

I could go on for hours and by God, I probably will...I always was a sort of a glutton for those good nights — — — Boy, sister you'd have me going around in circles with those "good nights" and then continuing to stand in the doorway — Just as I probably drove you to distraction by insisting you stay when you were dead weary and dreadfully bored — — oh well — call it love! —

No — no more — — you probably hear your mother coming, or perhaps the elevator so — — good night, sleep tight ...Know how much I adore you!!

Your
Sid

P.S. — — Some hasty note!!!

Worry about what Sid's role in combat would be was unremitting. Asked whether he was interested in trying for a commission as a pilot, bombardier, or navigator in the air force, he turned down the invitation in favor of the Chemical Warfare Service. "Just thought of something which may or may not interest you—This is a Chemical Warfare Service training center. Which means exactly what it implies—Servicing combat troops with Chemical Warfare apparatus—Repair of gas masks, preparation of gas bombs for artillery—servicing airplanes with poison gas. There is very little likelihood of any of us being used in front line fighting in any case—We probably will, however, be somewhere near the combat area—." The role of the Chemical Warfare Service and of the men in it became clearer to Sid over the next few weeks. Newly-named Chemical Warfare Battalions were being formed throughout the country, and Sid's company would be a motorized chemical mortar company. I wanted to know more about what this designation meant for his overseas service.

Thursday, 5:45 p.m.
June 11, 1942
Sweetheart,

I'm discouraged—definitely discouraged. I just did your fortune three times and three times that awful blonde came up closer to you than

I. And twice she had money and you had proposed. Please let me know when you meet this creature, so I can chase her to Libya, if necessary.

Girls remind me—have a good time Saturday night—but not very.

You still haven't told me what you will do "overseas." I have a dictionary, and I know what mortar means. Fella, please don't try to make anything sound better than it is. It'll be better if I'm prepared for the worst. Then think how happy I'll be when you come home...We'll take walks to Kanarsee with me over your shoulder after Fordham Road. We'll have long walks in the country, and long evenings on bear rugs in front of huge fireplaces in little inns with bad plumbing...but meantime let me know the worst. At least give me grounds for the fears that torture me.

You say I needn't be afraid of gas attacks in New York. Darling, I think there is a fundamental point you're missing—people are rarely afraid for themselves, for their own personal safety. I'm not afraid of gas attacks or of being blown up this minute. I assure you I wouldn't care —- simply because it would be impossible to. That's why you're not as fearful for yourself as I am – you couldn't be. Subconsciously or consciously you tell yourself that if you die you can't worry about it, and you couldn't even worry about me. I'm the only one in our combination to whom your existence is important. I know my existence isn't to me.

I'm not being morbid or emotional about this. I'm simply pointing out that my life is valuable to me only if you're around ....

Darling, do you know tomorrow's my birthday ? Eighteen, eighteen, eighteen....That should be a glorious age! Oh, Sid, I feel so much older than a year ago, so much more mature, so much more certain of what I want in life, and so much more discouraged about ever getting it. It isn't the exciting game I used to think it was. It's a treasure hunt with too many obstacles to make it any fun.

But I'm eighteen, almost the nicest age in the world...

I love you.

Estelle

Thursday (June 11) 8:00 P.M.

Good evenin' Sweet!

Oh Joy!! Heaven and the deep blue sea!! — Qualified in the use of pistol—astounded — ...Why am I so overjoyed?? — I don't know, —just that I hardly expected this to happen. — Qualifying doesn't label me as an "expert" or "sharpshooter" but since only 33% of men usually pass I feel quite cocky! — Labels me as a "marksman, second class gunner" in the pistol — means nothing — gives me the right to purchase and sport around one of those phony medals you see so often around the city — Don't think I will — — might send one home to mom and make her feel good!!! Can't say !!! —

In the above you have the complete picture of what happened today. We were awakened at 4:15, ate hurried breakfast and rushed to the pistol range. — — From 4:15 A.M. until 4:30 P.M. we were playing around with pistols. The actual time I spent in firing the pistol was not more than one hour. The rest of the time was spent coaching, loading clips, unloading used clips, running ammunition to firing line and so on. The heat was impossible to bear.

We've got the same thing in store for us tomorrow. We'll be awakened at 3:15 A.M. and spend the entire day on the rifle firing range. — We don't plan to get back until late Friday night hence I'm begging you to forgive me for not being with you the night of your 18th birthday — Congratulations, of course, — — my damned sincerest wishes that you have everything you want out of life — that includes me (I hope??) — — This August will be 4 yrs. — long time — lots of love — — loads of fun — — days of sheer pleasure — — Heck I wouldn't change it for all the money in the world. — — If a soldier can be permitted such a delicacy — It was "heavenly!"— I'm going to try my utmost to make it continue as such when I return —

Strange – I regret nothing I've done — — nothing we've done. — — Boy — I'd say that any man that hasn't been bit by the love bug just hasn't lived!!! — again — Happy happy birthday…

Well — 4 wk. preliminary training done with — Now comes more training in chemical weapons – 4.2 mortars, mines, projectors, gas grenades, candles, smoke pots, decontamination etc. a little on communications (I hope!) — Communications men train with this company! Nine more weeks of this — Since chemical weapons operate with the infantry — its necessary that we be as tough, if not tougher than the pebble-dusters — soo—ooo—Superman look out!!!…

Closing ——
I love you
Your
Sid

The training for the Chemical Warfare Service at Edgewood Arsenal became ever more arduous, but did not diminish our longing for one another.

19

Edgewood Arsenal
Co. G 2ⁿᵈ CWS Tng. Bn.
Maryland
(June 17, 1942)

Oh, Sweetheart how the army has failed – I'm supposed to be hardened. – to be impervious to gentle emotions, to be willing to shoot a man, like myself, without the slightest qualm – and, - - God, here I am so choked up with love that all I can do is sob out a sloppy I love you — love you —you—you…

When Mom and Dad left I walked into the woods alone and just sat there amongst the trees and mosquitoes thinking about you — being lonely for you — —Please please don't be unkind — I know I've no right to cry about loneliness—I know full well that I brought this upon myself— but 'Stelle if I didn't love you so damned much I'd never be troubled by it!!! — —You want me to tell you how I feel?—don't you??? Don't scold— Give a dumb soldier a break—okay??? …I'll come home, you needn't fear! … 'Stelle, I said I wanted to marry you and by heaven, and if there is a God, by God I'm coming home and if someone hasn't taken you by then officially with a license etc. — —I swear by all the hells a soldier can experience I'm taking you for my own.!!! I feel a part of you — — I can't get into this thing wholeheartedly because there is that part of me which you own!!! — — I can't feel reckless — — I can't be impatient — — I become cautious. — — You come between me and every wrong…

Look, sweet, we're not going to open up an inn — or did we inherit a fortune so that we could spend weeks at out-of-the-way inns!! With rotten plumbing no less!!!!

Concerning unscrupulous politicians and higher ups I have but this to say — — or at least I can repeat the general opinion of the military about this matter — — The soldier doesn't make wars — he ends them!!!

That's what we hope to achieve now — to finish this one as quickly as possible so that we may return to a half-way sane way of life without the constant insecurity and fear — — I'll grant that this false security may not last very long but at least we pray that with hard work, hard thinking and hard fighting we can enjoy a few years of normal living — — we pray???

Saturday morning after inspection I went to a motion picture training film concerned with the digging of foxholes, skirmish ditches, and trenches—nothing to say—except this comment—they insist it should take a soldier about thirty minutes to "dig-in." Sister—we all agree that when a man's caught in an open field with a machine gun spraying about he could be dug in and deeply in 60 seconds flat—

In the afternoon we had another class in decontamination work—The job of decontaminating New York City after a mustard attack would be a comparatively simple one—However in case of wooden houses the only safe method is to stand up-wind and burn the house to the ground—fascinating!!!!

This mustard's stuff no plaything—I went to visit a buddy in the hospital last evening and while there I saw a few of the Negroes that worked over at the arsenal who'd been burned by mustard—very, very, very disgusting, gruesome, extremely frightening affair.

Most of the men have already gone to bed—we've had quite a full two weeks. What with no Sunday off and three days at the range being awakened at 4 a.m. on those days we've had a pretty hectic time

I'll close now with love—lots of it.

Your

Sid

I was writing a paper for an English class on the philosopher William Godwin, who wrote, as I noted on one of my 3x5 cards, of "the delusion" with which young people entered marriage because of the circumstances of courtship. Sid had said that if he were assigned to a 4.2 mortar unit, I should "take those cards seriously."

2nd CWS Training Battalion
June 18, 1942
Tuesday, 12:30 p.m. – still on guard duty - now at Barracks - Barracks guard!!

Good afternoon sweet!!!

Well, here I am again with plenty of spare time – no more duty until change of guard at 4:30 p.m. — just sit around playing guard — sleeping — dreaming. About walking post last night — nothing much from 8 until 10 — Negroes very cheerful — would greet me with a smile and pleasant Hyah white boy!! — I smiled in reply — (not allowed to converse except in the line of duty!) —

I became strangely envious of these men. They're so easy-going. The colored men can bring their girls to camp and walk around freely. What I wouldn't do for just a few moments with you!!

After I was relieved there was a quick nap in the guardhouse—Was awakened again at 3:30 a.m. to walk post again.

'Stelle, I wouldn't exchange that 2 hour stretch for all the walks New York could ever offer.

Not a soul in sight—clear sky broken occasionally by flashes from Aberdeen proving grounds — complete silence except for booming at Aberdeen — I was conscious of nothing but myself and my footsteps —

'Stelle I won't try to put down on mere paper what went through my mind during those hours of being alone. Frankly, I found myself day-dreaming – day-dreaming of you. I could imagine myself holding you in my arms, kissing you, embracing you—you were there all the time—I once, a long time ago, called you "devil"—I said it then and repeat it—you're a devil!!!

You ask for a little clarification on some of these "puzzling" matters —Here's the facts: I'll be a member of a chemical mortar company. I will definitely not be an automatic rifleman or mortar man. (That, because of you)— I'm being trained for a position as a communications and staff man.

By the by, my dear, sweet Estelle—when I say you'd best begin taking those cards seriously I don't mean I want you to go off and marry someone else—By God, as you'll agree there's a limit to nobility!!

I realize, fully, the selfishness of this but heck, kid, I want you for myself— If, because of circumstances beyond our control we can't consummate our love by marriage—you can read 'em, feel miserable for a day or so and then throw the cards out—but as long as I'm alive and kicking—I'll come back to you—so help me!!! (Selfish cuss—but that's the way I feel!)

As for the danger — well — I'm a soldier now — I recognize no dangers — I'll be careful — Its all a matter of luck — where the shrapnel falls etc. — 'Stelle this may sound silly — but I'm going to ask you to come in on this gamble with me! Its sort of a game. If you win — one is just so much the richer — If you lose well — we're both good sports —— shrug your shoulders and say better luck next time!! —— In order to win though, it requires that you stick it out 'till the game's over.— I know you don't play games, I know I'm a bit out of character but I'm gently hinting that you wait for me — at least, give me a fighting chance when I come back! —— What the heck brought this on!! — That's what comes of too much leisure.

Truthfully, the picture is not as gloomy as you imagine —

I'm sure you can take of yourself – and while I'm around well — little devil — I'll take care of myself— sort of mutual!!

Your,

Sid

After a description of bivouac (partially included here) the subject of marriage was raised once again. The "Gordon," "Charles," "doctors," and "Sams" mentioned in the letter are characters from Eugene O'Neill's Strange Interlude. "Gordon" was the boy the heroine loved, killed in the first World War.

June 26

...After a most satisfying slumber Tuesday night we (I) had classes all morning — learned about cloud formations—cirrus, cirrus cumulus, strata cumulus — alto cumulus, alto cirrus, nimbus...etc. more discussion of wind velocity, temp, and humidity and its influence on chemical attack.

Then — then came the beginning of excitement — adventure — torture — painful tiredness — — an overnight bivouac.

When the company arrived at our camping grounds we immediately set up tents. Then C&S (communications and staff) set up telephone network to guard posts and headquarters — It was impossible to leave wire on ground with so many soldiers dashing about — consequently, I can say, beyond a shadow of a doubt that you'd have been thrilled to observe my apish technique as I shimmied up and down trees to set wire in branches!!...Considering the fact that as a 'youth' I'd never had the usual daring of the "young" and had never before climbed trees!!!

After the telephones were set we C&S men sat about and loafed — practiced a bit of semaphore and morse code — helped the commanding officer bring in equipment "staff" meaning general stooge for commanding officers — — ...

With the supper completed the entire group settled down to an old-fashioned outing spirit —— beer, pretzels, potatoe chips etc. were brought out by truck— Me with my simple single glass of beer — two pepsi-colas – and tons of potatoe chips!!...

The C&S men — all who were sober — spent the next few hours guarding the wires and telephone equipment from wandering boozers....

At ten the company left on an attack problem. No one was left in camp except the C&S men—consequently it was our responsibility to maintain a guard against any attackers camped nearby (It being the usual procedure to try and cut each others communication lines and sneak into other group's camp — dumping tents and disseminating many tear gas grenades.)...

I was relieved at 1:00 o'clock — slept for ½ hour and then took my turn at the switchboard until 4 o'clock A.M.—at 4:30 we, C&S, went with the commanding officer and laid a few mustard mine areas — blew them up. — This was for the benefit of practice for the rest of the men who were to try to discover and map mustardized (simulated) areas.

The rest of the day was practice in telephone and signal problems. At 3 P.M. I was taken from map-reading class and told I was on Battalion guard for the next day. — I was taken back in the lieutenant's car — I washed, shaved, dressed, drew pistol and paraded with other guards to guard house. — Walked post from 11 P.M. until 2 A.M. and 5:40 until 6:10 A.M. Am now Barracks guard writing the usual "too long" letter to the swellest girl alive!...

About the subject of Pros and Cons ... 'Stelle – we want to do the best thing — — you and I — the best thing for both of us — — Since little or nothing can be done for a soldier — It narrows down to a very simple fact — — We've got to do the best thing by our 'Stelle — — 'Stelle who fears her "Gordon" will die. Her "Gordon," who all the time expected to end up as a spineless Charles — I guess there's plenty of doctors and Sams wandering about — — But sweetheart its like I said — They'd better make it legal and even if it is legal they'd best see that you are very happy because as I've said on a thousandfold occasions I want you and will stop short of murder to get you — ...Be happy sweetheart — — tell me about school — Mike and Lenny are working in some camp — Lenny – silly idealistic adventurer like myself writes that he also is thinking seriously of joining up — — ...Oh yes — — Strange to hear Lenny tell me that you're broken up about my leaving — Where's that reserved 'Stelle I used to know so well...

It's about time for guard mount — got to clean up for tomorrows inspection — must phone you tonight if I can —

Lots of Love ——
I love you
Your
Sid

Sid refers to himself as "engaged" but it was not yet official

July 2

...This A.M. there was a long session in map-reading and map-making — We spent the morning drawing maps of the area — in the P.M. there was a practice setting up of mortar batteries and simulated fire!! — — I was stationed at the observation post with the second lieutenant — I see now why so many of them kick the bucket —

Tonight I read a bit — started and tore up bits of correspondence — decided to make application for officer candidate school (rest depends on precious sergeant and corporal) — Doubt very much whether I'll be successful —

'Stelle we've got to discontinue this cross-play — — You know what I mean — "It will only lead to bloodshed!" …

Really, I'm still happy — I'm glad you think enough of me to write long scathing scolding letters — I'd get worried, really worried, if there was nothing but stale friendly platitudes. — You're still my "gentleman" — aren't you???…

Enclosed you'll find cartoon that one of my buddies hung on the bulletin board — most interesting — I really can't see the resemblance between myself and any of them — so help me — all I dream of — when I dream is just a girl — not food, boats, or sleep, just one girl…

You're absolutely right about our financial status — I told you — I wanted to marry <u>you</u> for your money — nothing else — except perhaps — a bit of your beauty — a bit (very little) of your friendship — a whole grand hunk of your comradeship — — Your shoulder to sleep on — — Someone to sympathize with my poor sense of humor — — a pal — I wonder if the Lonely hearts club could pick me out one similar to that above if you should stop — impossible!!!

Concerning going out on night passes — I'm going to go home on a 36 hour pass once more — then I'll risk a few trips to Baltimore — strangely enough to see the museums — — you see I'm engaged to a young lady — — a lady whom I love dearly — love sufficiently enough not to have to run after "soldiers meat" — You see my love — I promised my love I'd come back — I said I loved her above everything else in the universe— — — I believe, my love, you realize I'm not the joking kind — — when I asked for marriage — I wasn't playing games — — I meant it seriously — When my sweet tires of me and casts me into the maelstrom then I'll begin hunting. Until then — "I'm happy!!"

> I love you.
> Your
> Sid

Missing Sid as I did, still broken-hearted that he had enlisted, I was not always an ideal correspondent. In this letter, he tells me so, with humor, but humor with a bite.

July 5

Sweet —

Have you ever encountered the untold and immeasurable brilliance of the locker A44 — There the ornate and fabulously beautiful Miss Estelle Spero resides. — High above the clothes, the ugly leggings, the books she lords. In her domain of Wildroot Hair Tonic and palmolive soap she mightily reigns — At each opening of her palace gates she greets the newcomer with the warmth and friendliness of the of the benevolent despot — To all who know but the shell she is the essence of loveliness and kindness — — But to those unfortunate underlings of her court who grovel at her feet — they know full well the wrath those dimples camouflage — They fear the lash of her biting censure — One, of her court,— the jester, suffers most — He strives endlessly and seemingly hopelessly to make her happy — Her only response is cynical haughtiness. One day she threatens to behead him — the next she entreats him to stand on his head and wiggle his ears "Oh if he would only do that – How happy she would be!!" Sorrowful jester, pitiable clown — how he sweats and strains — first he stands on his head but his ears don't wiggle, next he wiggles his ears but he can't stand on his head — — Never can he make his Queen happy—'Tis no use asking for an "E" for effort — Either he does it or — "To the Gallows!"

The jester's brow furrows with the creases of anxiety — How can he please his loved mistress — Is there no substitute — Oh would he were a knight with shining armor and a draft deferment — Then he could be with his love — Then he could lounge beside her — — courting her — — Would he had wealth ($900 to be exact) to shower presents at her feet (or her middle finger) — Position — reputation — All he has, lonely jester, is unfailing loyalty and a desire, but not the means, to make her happy. — — Poor- Poor – Pauvre jester — —

End of silly story — — It started out normally enough — its this new pen of mine — just runs into these things — — oh darling — I do do do do — love you....

To punctuate my paragraphs I'll simply say I love you ————

Did you know that the army now runs on a 24 hour clock...Why??? — I'm sure I don't know!! I love you.

My Dad came to visit me today. I'm afraid he thought me a bit morose and sulky — Couldn't help it — Can't stand being asked questions continuously — I just stopped talking after a while — He wanted to give me some money when he found out what I had left — I'm afraid I insulted

26

him when I refused— I can't stand people who try to press things on me
— — Nuts — I love you.

I just completed "Goodbye Mr. Chips," Hilton —…am now starting
"Lost Horizon" also Hilton — — There's where our money goes — those
25c pocket volumes.

I'll confess that rotten stupid jerk that I am I allowed myself to be
talked into playing a game of cards — You know that good old Diamond
Luck — wham — went $7 to the other world — I love you.

I've still got enough so don't sympathize — If I'm that unintelligent as
to get into a game like that I'll have to suffer the consequences and go in
for a little more economy — I've made a solemn vow — never to borrow
from anyone — not even my parents — — I love you.

Help me will you and give me a sound scolding for my gross
inconsideration for "our" money — so help me — I must be still lucky in
love cause I'm sure as the devil unlucky at cards — See what you do —
There — now I've made it all your fault!!! — I love you.

Well — sweetheart — I'll have to bid you adieu — — and don't be
anything but happy — …

Rumor has it we'll be going on one of those phony midnight maneuvers
again — oh well.

Darling I'll close with love.—

Your Sid

July 10 10:20 P.M.

…Its still raining — I go on guard duty from 12 (24:00-03:00) until 3
A.M. It will rain then too — I'll spend the weary wet hours thinking about
you — worrying about your welfare — Dream about you — How much I
love you — How unworthy I am of the faith you have in me — how cruel
I've been to you — — I'll think about the home, nice defense job, draft
deferment, complacency — then I'll become conscious of the dampness
— the wet clothes — the dripping water down my neck — the mud —No,
I won't regret it — not at all —I'm happy — absolutely ——I know what
I'm doing and why I'm doing it — The issues will not be argued at this
point —

'Stelle — — — — …

Seriously, darling, I do have to call it a day — I don't know how I can
walk post tonight. I'm dead tired — I guess the rain'll keep me awake. —

Excuse any nonsense in this correspondence — I really am not in full
possession of my faculties —

I love you

Your

Sid

The next day's letter described what it was like to walk guard in the constant rain, and what he was thinking about.

July 11

...Rain, Rain, endlessly pouring violent rain . The wind lashed the waves of drops against the nearby barracks — head low, face dripping, feet soaked and mud covered a bedraggled lonely figure battled the enraged elements — In one hand he held the butt of his pistol, in the other — — an onion! — He was happy — There he was, with no chance of going home to his loved one —— with no chance of "losing face" by onion breath ...

You get the general idea?? — Before going on post I happened into the kitchen to get a few "tid-bits" to keep my spirits up. Everything was locked, consequently I grabbed all nearby that wasn't nailed down — net result of scavenger hunt — two raw frankfurters, two jam sandwiches, 7 plums, 3 onions ...

As quickly as the rain started — it stopped 02:00 — for the last hour the subdued, valiant, drenched "sinner" shivered and shook as the winds came...

Oh the tortures we soldiers undergo!! — It really wasn't bad — Don't hand me an "I told you so!" — I enjoyed it. — — Had a glorious time thinking about you — Regardless of what you may think or say or do — I still love you — so there — You've attached yourself to a good-for-nothing onion addict — see???...

Sweetheart — in my last letter, I'm not certain what I wrote — I was sort of weary and dizzy —...

I'm certain you are aware that I'm now stalling — stalling that final good-night — just to be with you an extra few moments —

You can take that physics in your stride—

I always knew your interest in me was purely selfish — I tell my sweetheart, the girl I'd die for (Don't pick that out and use it for a good three pages of scolding — you did it before) that I can't come in to see her. — Does she sob in loneliness for want of me — Does she say, "Darling, how I want you and you alone!" not at all — just a simple ——"Now who's going to do my physics homework for me!!"

Oh love — why grind your bayonet against my ribs! —...

You know when a bayonet is thrust into a man's chest it sometimes gets stuck in the ribs or some other hard section — In order to get his bayonet out the soldier will sometimes fire his rifle — the bullet enlarging the hole made by the bayonet— thus facilitating its removal — —

28

Well, darling, there we have our relationship in a nutshell — I've got you deep within me — imbedded within my heart, body, mind — Its stuck there —...

Look, while we're talking along these lines — I fully realize the so-called pressure that some alleged princesses (wenches as far as I'm concerned) may put upon your faith in my love —'Stelle — we've gotten along as free-thinking minds — capable of knowing our own minds — respecting each others faults, whimsies and desires — — I'd like you to make up your own mind — clearly and thoughtfully —

Remember an incident a while ago with a Muriel Wagg — I said I didn't care to walk with anyone who distrusted me — — That's the way it is now. I dislike this new attitude intensely — say, perhaps, that I've betrayed our love — that I've been cruel, unthinking, selfish, unkind — true — but —— 'Stelle don't doubt my love for you — — never!! – whatever you do!!! Charge, toss me out — but know I love you.

'Stelle —— oh —— well— nothing else — I love you—

You see what hours of leisure do to people —-I couldn't sleep anyway—this kind of week-end tired feeling needs your shoulder, so, consequently — no sleep —...

Listen, darling, something has gone through today which makes me very happy indeed— Another one of my promises I made to you has gone unbroken — Nothing may come of it but my promise was to try!! Don't ask me what it is — It may never materialize — Don't think about it (deep dark mystery) like that pass I expected today — Nothing at all may come of it.

Say—Don't you think this has gone far enough — I do! — I'll have to be dogmatic about this — so-long until tomorrow — I love you

Your

Sid

...If nothing comes of this officers candidate application – its pretty safe to say that within a few months I'll get a corporal's rating $66 and later perhaps a sergeant's $95 —

Oh, that deep dark secret — you might as well get in on it — Its been going on now for about three weeks — During which I or rather my mother got a transcript of my college credits — three letters of recommendation — birth certificate — endless applications — — Its an attempt to get into the Air Corps ground crew as a communications man — — Now look — the papers are on their way to Washington — Then there'll be a physical to worry about if Washington passes it which I doubt very very much — All this will take oodles of time — I may be over the waves before anything, even the refusal, comes through — Then, there comes the final guillotine ——a board exam — oh — previous to this is another one of those damned I.Q. affairs — The board's going to ask a lot of questions — — questions — — questions — you know how I hate questions — Especially when I haven't the slightest conception of what the inside of a radio looks like — I can turn dials beautifully but I guess they don't want dial turners — —This may take months — so, if I were you, I'd do exactly what I'm doing — forget about it — — And another promise bit the dust! —

Darling — I love you —

Finally – goodbye — until tomorrow

Sid

The strain of hoping for a week-end pass was beginning to tell on Sid.

July 13

  …This continual strain and worry about a pass is getting me down — This morning I was a table waiter — after the inspection was completed — we received 86% (88% passing) — we were threatened with loss of all chances at getting passes for the week-end — I almost keeled over. Between swallowing lumps I began growing angry — angry for being so much in love that I was afraid to answer back for fear of loss of pass — It was the same last week — When names were taken for week-end passes I was off in the field drawing maps with the Communication and Staff men — No explanations, no entreaties could budge the corporal's decision — … 'Stelle I have no temper to speak of, but sweetheart, I'm beginning to simmer — I pray I don't boil over — —…

  Look, darling, my "wild dashes" as you refer to them are merely moments of silence — you know how I abhor silent moments — In ordinary conversation I'd be whistling, imitating a train or thinking about whether or not you were having a good time and always arriving at a negative answer — Somehow I never was satisfied with the job I was doing…

  Sweetheart — Don't go off so with your Dad — no need for it — — You know whatever you do will be okay — — But — well — selfish little Sid wants to see 'Stelle — wants to see her badly — come down Sunday — Do homework and stuff Friday or something. If I don't get that pass — please please — come down —

  I'll quit now — good night darling — I love you.

Your

Sid

On July 18 Sid had an afternoon pass, arrived at my house with roses, and we spent a wonderful evening in Manhattan, even going to a night club, something we had never done before and never did again. Many men from Edgewood had already been "shipped out" and the question of when Sid's turn would come hung over us.

(July 20)

…Rumors are flying fast and ferociously through the entire company. — I say simply — I'll believe it when it happens!! …it's only that these damned annoying rumors and gossip make it seem that we will have to face each other across a wedding ring a lot sooner than either of us planned — perhaps there may not be any opportunity — 'Stelle darling, sweetheart for both our sakes, make absolutely certain you're not suffering from 'uniformitis' — …We get hitched, not because of what may or may not happen to me, but because we both love each other and sincerely desire a future together — make sure you're not influenced by passionate embraces, long hours together, or my "money" (???) — …

Aw damn!! — now I'm certain people are watching me — Every time someone calls my name a non-commissioned officer walks over and says — "So you're Diamond!" — Nuts! — I'm not interested — I'm not interested — I won't worry about it any longer — I'll try for my stripes and call it a day!

I'll close sweet — with that ocean of love that swells and rocks my poor insides — By heavens, I can't walk around with that "hungry" feeling all the time. Think of my "weight" and the other 7 people at my table!! —

> I love you
> Your
> Sid

July 25

…This morning my platoon — (oh — it is now the 4th platoon —) — that special potential officer candidates group I spoke about —— underwent the most exacting inspection we've yet experienced. Every corner was examined for dust— the soles of the shoes were examined for dust — stones in the holes of the heels were cause for a gig — meticulous inspection of lockers …the inspection lasted two and one half hours!!…

By the by — when [your mother] does answer my flirtatious billet doux — We've got much in common — we both love the same "item" — both desire its happiness — both want the "thing" to be spared the knocks and scrapes of shipping along the road of life — One wants to protect it by not letting it out of the shop — by keeping it from inconsiderate handlers — The other thinks this product is constructed so finely and sturdily that it can withstand the shocks of existing — of life!!

You see — — — I'll close now — praying that you'll be here tomorrow — hope, hope, hope —

> I love you
> Your
> Sid

The next day, when I did indeed visit, we once again discussed marriage, and whether Sid should accept OCS if it was offered. In the next letter, he wrote, "I imagine we have reached a stalemate — both digging in for a bit of 'trench warfare' — the old questions about should or shouldn't — nuts!!"

July 30

...What's happened since last I wrote—...

In the afternoon I went down to see our Captain — — He interviewed a group of us who were applying for O.C.S. (Officer Candidate School). — He asked me questions relating to 1. map reading, first aid, care, construction, and use of gas mask, construction of the 0,3 Springfield rifle, personal background. — Result — He approved my application and sent it on —

Now comes a more intensive interview by a screening board which judges one on every phase of military knowledge, also personal appearance, attitude, habits! — Questions concerning political views etc. make up a substantial part of this interview — If one is successful here (which will probably be negative in my case — I'm a bit shaky about the whole thing) then comes a careful physical examination.

I'm hoping — hoping — that's all I can do — Besides its other advantages it does mean another 3 months near home — Oh well — If I make it — okay, if not okay too...

Good night darling — Don't worry about me — I'm not worth it — — Too much stupid pride! — I know it now — ...You'll never have to worry about it though — Everything leaves me when I'm with you — pride, temper, anger, — just melt — see what I mean —...

> I love you,
> Your
> Sid

I was not jubilant about the possibility of Sid's being chosen for Officer Candidate School. "If being an officer means increased danger, it isn't worth that much (snap of the fingers here)." Sid had decided to apply nevertheless. My desire for his safety clashed with his resolve.

(August)

...I beg you not to think too harshly of me for going ahead this way — I didn't enlist in order to find a safe, warm, post to loaf about in...

Sweet, I love you — you can't change that — not for a while anyway — all I ask — well you know — let's do it gracefully if it ever has to come! Sweet, no one, nowhere, could possibly mean so much to me as you do except perhaps my parents — I recognize no differences in our worlds — I see no argument between us — The construction of a terrific barrier — one of ideals, opinions, etc. is pretty flimsy to say the least — There's little a soldier miles from the scene of action can do to help the situation — There isn't much I can do — It's all up to you — to the extent to which you feel for me — to that damned intangible called love!! I don't want you to think our friendship has to be continued by force — the friendship can never pass on — The love — well ——if it required the close presence of both individuals — both humbling themselves to the will of the other — If it could survive only with the continued weekly visits, letters, flowers, etc. — there isn't much to it — is there? It's like we both said — "We know our own minds and what we want!" — I know how I feel towards you — I know I love you — I've never gone to Baltimore as yet. No one else holds the slightest interest for me —— This goes well into the realm of insanity — forgive it all —

> I love you.
> Your
> Sid

We considered ourselves "engaged-to-be-engaged" and Sid had the temerity to call me his "fiancée."

August 13
Hello Sweet! —

...By the by – I'm writing this letter before supper—first time in a long while I've had a few moments to devote to my "fiancee"—you know it comes easy now!——previously I'd gag at it every time it became necessary to describe our relationship. My first instinct would usually be to blurt out "girl friend!"—Then I'd stop, think a minute—contemplate saying "lady friend" and finally end up shrugging my shoulders and stumbling through a "fiancée"!—Delightfully refreshing affair if I must say so myself—I'll have to recommend it to all my friends as a sure panacea of all mental as well as physical ills—…

Curiosity about my fate doesn't bother me in the least—Ship me anyplace, anywhere, anytime—only please not at an arsenal!!—…

Fellows are leaving gradually. They're going in small groups now but we expect to go in larger numbers this week-end—the idea being that we all will be out by Tuesday!!

Sounds peculiar to hear myself shouting the same platitudes as the soldiers ride off—

"See ya in Tokio!!"—"Save Hitler's moustache for my razor!!"—"Keep on the beam!!" "Let us know where you are!!" —That group that left last week—impregnating outfit—is already somewhere on the ocean….

I've just been glancing at my handwriting—If you bother deciphering this stuff you must be in love—although, secretly, I suspect you just count the number of pages—and whisper to yourself—if its four or more—He still loves me—less than four— "the cad!!!" (you'd probably be right!)

As a matter of general interest you might be interested in the history of those mad dashes you see thrown wildly about in my letters—… Confidentially the only real reason for the adaptation of this system is because of my damned laxity in punctuation. It certainly saves thought— Besides I write as I think and I don't think with punctuation on my mind— What mind??—Who started this—…

I love you

Your

Sid

While writing this letter, Sid still did not know whether he would make OCS.

August 15

Hello Sweet!

I have your letter of Thursday the 14th — You make many inquiries — I shall strive earnestly to make things clear to you once and for all — If I don't succeed — well — I don't succeed!…

Sweetheart nothing is definite in the army — a soldier can never be sure of anything At present I may be classified as a bottle washer in a Laboratory company or a reconnaissance corporal in a 4.2 mortar company

— Je ne sais pas!! All will be cleared up, definitely, by next Wednesday — That's the last day my company will be at Edgewood.

You mention the fact that you're the cynic of this pair — sister — move over!!! — 'Stelle I expect nothing more from my "friends" than what I've given and would be willing to give to them in the way of time, comradeship, loyalty — Let us, rather, brush it off with this rationalization — they probably didn't understand the physical and mental tortures I, as well as the others, was undergoing at that time — Mind you I don't put my case up as a singular occurrence — Everyone here had to undergo the process of changing from an independently thinking individualist of mediocre physical strength to a well disciplined, hardened, automaton willing to throw himself into the enemy without thought of death!! It wasn't easy — we bucked, fought, cried, shouted, — we learned never to volunteer for anything, we learned how to goldbrick, how to save our energies by loafing through boondoggling jobs. — We learned how to hate! — Look, I'm not attempting to salt old wounds — my only concern at present is to live through this thing and attempt to make up to you for all the anxieties, discomfort I may have caused you. —

Sweetheart I've never even thought of accusing you of being cruel but 'Stelle when you say I'd 'probably be <u>delighted</u>' if I were sent overseas! — enough said!!! — Someday, perhaps, you'll awaken to the fact that I don't like you, I don't merely enjoy your company, I'm not too interested in just friendship — Someday you'll realize that I <u>love</u> you, passionately, ardently, irrevocably — — the day of "you go your way I go mine" has passed as far as we're concerned — your hurts are 50% mine, your worries, anxieties belong in no small part to me — My main concern is to attempt to make you happy — if, because of circumstances, not now — later — but, hell, 'Stelle, the days you write of having a good time, of doing something which proves interesting are my easiest here at Maryland — It's the truth — Your happiness gives me peace of mind —

You see!!!!

——Don't ever make me flare up like that again — its about time you were conscious of the fact that whatever love you have for me is being returned twofold — one might even say thricefold (if such an expression exists!!) — fascinating, isn't it, this love!! …

In reference to your dislike of the use of the bayonet — you're absolutely correct — It is well said that the "meek shall inherit the earth." One can always seek a "Shangri-la" in which to hide oneself from the hardships of living — of existing with strife and turmoil — that's more than true. It is, however, the "brutes," as they are occasionally referred to, who battle against the oppression of the meek…

35

But — frankly — a person can live a complete life seeking and perhaps finding "escape" — I, who essentially was always an escapist have whirled (a bayonet manipulation where you run away from foe and suddenly turn)…

I'm going to close.

> I love you.
> Your
> Sid

That evening, Sid telephoned to say that he had been rushed into a class—not even allowed to pack or change clothes. Of the forty men who had been considered for OCS, Sid was one of the three who made it. Training continued until mid-November. He was able to come to New York on several week-ends.

August 20

Hello Darling —

…Say, darling, you've got into the limelight in this tent — Either our relationship is so singular or my method of presenting it is unique — Imagine them turning off Jack Benny in favor of listening to my description of my week-end with you!!! — … these people don't understand — … They tease the happy smile I wear on Mondays — They envy my energy on Sunday nights — They growl at my dreamy attitude Monday morning —

Well, I am in love, hopelessly, foolishly, gloriously!! They can heckle from now till doomsday — I like it this way…

Silly letter — Silly guy

> I love you
> Your
> Sid

Sid had come in the week-end before the following letter.

Sept. 22

…Left you 10:15 — train left 20 minutes late! Seated next to a young lady — name– Mary– NYU graduate psych major …We talked until I dropped off to sleep — very rude I'll agree but 'c'est la guerre' or something. Arrived in Baltimore 2:00 A.M.

A mad dash by taxi through the stilled streets of Baltimore to the Greyhound Bus station — Arrived at station 2:15 — no taxi could take me to Edgewood — Dilemma? You're not kiddin' — hopped aboard a Greyhound bus (2:55 A.M.) bound for New York— Had the driver let me off at a crossroads four miles from camp. — 3:45 — — Time now grew shorter — a race — time and myself in the hush of the early morning — Then ensued a silent gasping dash — The only sound was the pat of my toes against the asphalt — in between heaves I'd glance up to the sky. — Peculiar — I kept searching for the big dipper. Had to be in camp at 5:00 A.M. Rush, Hurry! Got into camp at 4:45A.M.. — A "Frank Merriwell" photo finish! Slept until Reveille 5:20. —...

One of the swellest things I've yet experienced — surpassed only by your generosity and friendship! When I arrived I found my bed made and all set for a comfortable snooze — John Horan had made my bed for me in anticipation of my late arrival! — 'Stelle, if you knew the army, that's an unusual gesture of friendship!

I'll quit with love —
Sid

The question of whether to marry had come up again, and my indecision was painful for both of us.

Sept. 27

...As is my wont ...when I'm too weary to walk, too disgusted to read, too ugly to write — I stepped into the chapel — ...

While seated there, alone, in the strange hush that only religion can bring about, the thought of death overcame me. — Peculiar, unique situation. — Never before had it ever entered my mind. It was not fear or religious dread that overwhelmed me but a burning curiosity about life, living, and passing on — The smallness of myself and every individual in this wild chaotic universe was so apparent!

I picked up the bible — opened it ——"Deliver me from mine enemies, Protect me from them that persecute me." I smiled and thought of Lieutenant D. as my persecutor. — Thoughts of the Japanese and the "war of annihilation" made whirlpools in this usually stable mind of mine — Destruction, fires, explosions all kept pounding within me — a unique battle this one. — The Germans may crack but the Japanese will have to be crushed, utterly and irrevocably ("Time") —

What a guy will think about when he's alone!! —

As for you and I — well — it did get the customary mulling over. A warrior (potentially) seldom thinks in terms of moonlight, stars, romance — He must be coldly practical — calculating, — assured. Before he makes a move he must be certain of his "security" — He must never be surprised — on guard all the time! In case of attack there should be a prearranged "alternate position" to which he may retire. Being a military man, of sorts, my thoughts generally run in that direction — Indecision is what causes men to die! Consequently the soldier learns to make a hasty "estimate of the situation" and decide his course of action immediately! A soldier enjoys people with decisive ways. Individuals who don't worry and confuse — who know what they believe, and what they want! Its not a scolding, nor a reprimand — Its just that I'd like you to know what you want to do and do it!!! —

Me??? — — life is boring without you — even if its only thoughts of you!! — true, I can feel age creeping unto me by leaps and bounds — so many things I enjoyed, loved, seem like "kid stuff." — I can safely say that the only thing that has survived this metamorphosis has been my love and friendship towards you. — ...

You've been so kind and good to me swell, cute 'Stelle — you sort of take my breath away! —Be happy!

> I love you.
> Your,
> Sid

I expected to graduate from Hunter College in June and wondered what I would then be able to contribute to our struggle to win the war.

Sept. 29
Hello Darling!

... 'Stelle I believe firmly and honestly that the most valuable thing you could possibly do in this wearisome struggle is to stick to your studies. This is going to be a dull, dreary, bestial, cruel world when this conflict is over. Its individuals like yourself who must fight the greatest battle of them all to maintain, preserve, and foster the "humanities." The warrior's fight is simple — He battles the mud, weather, disease, lice — He kills tangible beings! — Yours is a more complex struggle — Not everyone must close their minds to thought, to beauty, love, literature — In this cruel vortex of blood and slaughter your job will be to keep gentleness of mind and expression from sinking to the dark depths of vulgar inconsiderate existence —

I'd like you to consider your battle as vital to the prevention of world chaos as I believe mine!!!...

I still love you.
Must close now.

Your
Sid

Oct. 24, 1942
Sweetheart!

Allow me to introduce a most wretched person – he calls himself Sid
– what others call him is best not discussed amongst gentlemen – This chap
stands 5 feet 9 inches – weighs 170 lbs – dirty blonde (very dirty) – ruddy
complexion – good posture – polished shoes – glistening belt buckle – closely
shaved – In fact the epitome of what a good soldier should look like —Yet
he still gets a demerit—what for???—Dirty finger nails!!!!

This after he'd scrubbed and brushed the damn things (all ten of them)
for ten minutes in the A.M. — 5 others received gigs for biting nails – a good
deal for haircuts —

Sid, though, has to get pinched on the basic fundamentals!!…

Training at OCS was almost over.

Nov. 1
Hello Sweet !! —

This is a most unique situation — Think of it — a whole study period
with nothing to study — tomorrow we go on an 8 hour tactical "walk" of
17 miles. This will include a great deal of the terrain we've been milling
over in our map problems. We will determine once and for all the debatable
question of whether or not Winters Run is fordable — This will be done by
frequent crossings and wadings etc.—

I'm in one of those peculiar moods — halfway between loneliness and
anxiety — — oh well —

Sweetheart, I've got the swellest pair of parents any fellow could
possibly be blessed with — why bring this up?? — I don't know, its just that
my inherent reticence forbids my telling this to them and I just want to talk
about it. — Ye Gods, they've done everything in the world for me — — I
can't even imagine the methods I might use to demonstrate my gratitude and
affection — — I swear by all that's holy I'll never do anything to make them
ashamed of me — whether I live or die they're going to [be] proud of me —
My mother will always have the opportunity to say proudly — " my son did
such and such" — Don't mind the above — its just that I'm overcome by the
response I've received from them at every request or even hint of desire on

39

my part — Its helped me a good deal through the hell of the past six months — It will help me in my future duties —

Please forgive my spouting off this way — I know its probably of little interest to you, but its your misfortune to be my "wailing wall"! — the pal, the friend, the comrade to whom I may entrust my innermost thoughts, angers, hates. — Without you — "rien!" — Every time I receive your letter... it brings on a glow of comfort — of knowing some one is standing by. That all connections to the past have not been severed — — —

Of all the unhappy luck I've been picked to act as a sergeant (this is not definite) for the graduation parade — I'll probably be trailing in the rear of some company in the review — but an appointment — small as it is — strongly indicates that there is at least a small degree of confidence in my "command presence" — This job received because most of the pet stooges flunked a subject or two — which automatically disqualifies them from these positions regardless of tactical officer's recommendation. Oh, politics where shall you cease!! —

Things look a bit on the brighter side — although I still maintain that a cautious attitude of " perhaps I'll receive the commission" would be best — Gosh darn it !! — I almost failed a map problem because of that stupid cautious "attitude" — I had insisted on maintaining a reserve force while the school solution required that all guns be used — I refused to commit my reserves. The school asks that they be used in certain instances. I balk at leaving suicide holding forces — School insists all barriers be covered by fire power. Oh dear.

Tuesday night we go on a "pleasant" night problem — I pray we don't suffer the same torture the ninth class went through. Besides being forced to crawl for hours through cold wet rain-soaked ground about 50% of them had their faces infected with poison ivy — resulting from a crawl through ivy patch with face close to ground. — For one week they presented the most amazing sight — men masked in calamine lotion unable to shave — twitching faces (unable to move hand to scratch while at attention!!) —...

I love you, my love, I love you — silly — but heck — I do ...

I love you

Your

Sid

Mrs. Diamond and I went together to Sid's graduation as a second lieutenant. We were proud of his achievement, but not happy to learn that he was being assigned to Fort Bliss, Texas for further training in a weapons unit. His uniform, particularly his hat, his formal manner before enlisted men, my trepidation for the future— all contributed to my feelings of strangeness, of unreality.

On leave, just after graduating from OCS

During his ten days of leave, which he spent at home before going to Texas, we were once again able to see friends, take long walks, and talk, talk, and talk, to renew and reinforce our love. His mother invited us to a festive dinner at a Russian restaurant, Kretchma, on 14th Street, where we enjoyed each other's company, good food, and great music, and where we stored up memories for the uncertain future.

Sid left for Texas on November 24, by train, from Pennsylvania Station, and there followed a journey of six days, recounted in his letters. The landscape of Texas, with its sand and dust, provided a new, not entirely pleasant, experience.

Dec. 1

The Lord, enraged, punishes his flock. With angry breaths he blows violently. The wind lashes over the desert. It carries the sharp tiny dust particles swiftly through the camp. They sting the soft faces of the humans who dared invade their homes. The dust crawls everywhere. — In shoes, down backs, noses stuffed with sand. The dry dirt seeps through the walls. Nothing can hold it back. White pillows coated with sand — faces reddened by the pounding of the earth — It is impossible to keep one's eyes open. — Some men put on their grotesque dust respirators. They walk around like prehistoric monsters. Others, not having their respirators handy don their gas masks. All the above rhetoric boils down to an old fashioned desert sand storm!

The work in this place is extremely "trying." — Yep — I walk around all day watching other men work — seeing to it that they do work. — Supervise the non-commissioned officers who do all of the instructing. My daily schedule, so far, is as follows. — — Arise to the music of the 82 Horse drawn field artillery band. That's at 6:30 A.M. — Dress, shave, shower, etc.. No — don't make bed or clean up — orderly does that, (we pay him $3 each a month) — At 7:00 A.M. I stand outside trying to get a lift to my company. Arrive at co. 7:45 eat — loaf until 9:00 — then walk around doing nothing until dinner — more doing nothing until supper — and then supper and home — at 6:00 P.M. — a shower to get rid of those sand particles. Then letters, reading, talking etc.

Perhaps we can write a bit about the trip through Texas — Played Gin Rummy with Ruth — traveling all the way from New Jersey to live with her husband (soldier boy) Ate Turkey Thanksgiving meal with Lieutenant Blum (nurse), Ruth, another Lieutenant who was a veteran of Pearl Harbor, Bataan, Corregidor, had been wounded several times. Interesting talk then back to Pullman to sit and watch the scenery go by.

We came upon a large oil field. — Oil wells jutting skyward for miles on end extending beyond the horizon — Dirty smelly, oily towns, shacks that we would call hovels serve as homes for these people.

Next we'd be astounded by a tremendous expansion of nothingness. — perfectly flat plains for as far as the eye can see. Just lonesome empty earth. — at long intervals we'd come upon tumbled-down unpainted dirty gray homes. Poor Ruth would turn white — for fear that she might have to live in a place like that. We took full advantage of her fears and teased her pointing out so-called "ideal" homes for herself —

Cotton fields at intervals — straight rows of low bushes. Many of the fields still unpicked blossomed with blots of white cotton balls. — All these going to waste for lack of pickers. Here we'd see a warehouse with stacks and stacks of cotton balls — There was another oil well — In the distance we could see a tree — mountains appeared far in the horizon —

We go through another stretch of barren Texas soil — cactus blooms everywhere, dry, stone studded earth — once or twice we pass through a forest — a forest of short crooked trees. I put a wager of $5 to be paid if we saw one straight tree — I still have the money — — You know I always bet on sure things! — This was barren Texas — miles and miles of God's forsaken country.

The cattle of Texas were a big disappointment to me — perhaps it's the time of the year. — Thin, scrawny, ragged beasts they wandered from one green spot to another. Bones protruding — sad eyes — These were not the fat steers of Tom Mix picture shows. Supper — more turkey — then to bed.

The wind is howling outside — at each new gust it seems to whisper — 'Stelle — 'Stelle —As it whistles around the corner of the building I get the queerest sensation of longing for my own love — a strange yearning for an unexplainable something which can only be you — sweetheart, I love you —

> Your
> Sid

(Dec. 7)

…Saturday night something happened which I've always contended took place only in the movies or only happened to the other guy! Saturday Lieutenant Sherrel, (medic) and his wife and Lts. Margelies and Banterro (also medic) and I went for a spree in Juarez — Subsequent to a lengthy discussion of where to go and what to do we finally ended up in the "Casanova" — The meal was excellent — The drinks? — didn't have enough to comment — Then the floorshow !!! — ah that floorshow!! — my reputation!! — my reticence!! — my prestige — all — all lost — lost in the horrible vortex of notoriety!! — The horror!! But, — let me get on with the story!

We suffered through some has-been American songstress and danseuse (or somethin') called "The Bowery Belle" — No attention need be paid to the gross lack of talent! Argentina was next represented by three male singers — How do I know they came from Argentina??? — They sang in a tongue which I "instantly" recognized as Argentian Spanish — Also there was the fact that they were billed as the "three Argentinians"!! — They were good!! — The M.C. drooled through some songs and then came my doom!!! —

Two Spanish dancers went through violent wild contortions in typical Spanish dances — Aside we might mention that motion pictures can't possibly substitute for the real thing. — Exciting, blood-warming, fast pounding dances. The savage beating of the heels shook the room — The roar of the clacking castanets — The whirling, swirling senorita. This was burning madness!! —

After completing two dances she and her partner waited while the audience urged them to return — My friends (???) urged her to do the "Flirtation" dance. While my back was turned my friends (???) pointed me out to the senorita!! — There I was quietly watching the dance seated in a "ring-side" seat.

She advanced toward me. It soon became obvious that I was the object of her "flirtation." As she danced around me, her partner made angry gesticulations — slammed the table — snapped his castanets in my face. — Suddenly, she sat down in my lap — no, no wait — that's not all — She planted three beautiful red gooey kisses on my face — making me look like the comedian after a session with his girl — — no — no — there's more — hold your seat. She then lifted me bodily from my chair (I was too astonished to resist!) and pulled me around the dance floor with her — dancing all the time (much to the delight of my comrades (???) — The senorita then carried me off in the direction of her dressing room — no — she let me go at the door. —

As a consequence of all this everyone I meet remarks "I hear you got a contract at the Casanova" — or— "Since when do you do Spanish dances?" —

What a life — what a life ?????..

Perhaps you're interested in the simple procedure of crossing the Mexican border across the Santa Fe bridge — It seemed fascinating to me at the time —

After taking a cab or the trolley one is deposited at the American side of the Rio Grande (Grand River, my foot! — a mud creek as far as I could see!! —) One then changes all one's currency into 2 dollar bills and change — This "courtesy" is offered at the price of one penny on the dollar. — Proceeding through the gate we are stopped by the intelligence officer —

"What's your citizenship?"

"American!" — Simple — then onward to the customs officials and more intelligence officers.

"Got any letters, papers, photographs?"

"No!" (Here is where I had to destroy two letters addressed to you in order to get across!)

Passing through this gauntlet of questions we are accosted by an M.P. — Here we show our "Good Conduct" Pass —

A Good Conduct pass entitles all those who hold them to remain in Mexico until 11:00 P.M. — If one misbehaves these passes are taken away.

Once through this ordeal we come to the toll station where we deposit the astounding sum of two cents!...

This is the trip across — Crossing the bridge on the way home is very similar — the exception perhaps is that when traveling over the bridge the second time one pays only <u>one</u> cent...

I'll close now with love, affection — "amiga mia" — (friend of mine) — "<u>A usted amo</u>" (I love you)

Your
Sid

Dec. 12

My sweet!!

No matter how hard I try I always get "officer of the day" when something's cooking. This evening has been cool, so far — No drunk explaining his approaching insanity — no brawl in the P.X. — — But — Tonight's Saturday night — <u>the</u> night — The only special work I've done so far has been to answer numerous phone calls and to act as go-between for the colonel — a major and the Plans and training officer — it gets complicated after awhile — we got by, though. Also received emergency call from red-cross to get extension of furlough for soldier with sick wife — — so far — — so good!

Here's something which may or may not be of interest...

You'll recall I mentioned the curfew hours for soldiers of the third army — you remember — must be off the streets week-days at 11:00 P.M. and in camp by 11:30. On Saturday night that's extended to 2: A.M. — Also must be out of Mexico by 11:00 P.M. every night. — Added to these restrictions a flock of new ones have been imposed on the soldiers — This resulted, primarily, from an increase in venereal infections —

With the cooperation of the Mexican police it has been so stipulated that all soldiers discovered in the vicinity of known houses of prostitution will be put under arrest. — That's not too bad — wait till you hear the rest.

Any Mexican woman found walking with a U.S. soldier in Juarez must be able (by some mysterious, unknown means) to prove to the Mexican police that she's not after "carnal delights" — (what sarcasm- it slays me!!) — If she can't prove this — either by friends or identification papers she'll be arrested — It's the God's honest truth — — To quote a private in my company

"I met the gal in El Paso — We thought we'd drop into Juarez to eat — We're not there more than half an hour when up pops a Mexican cop and starts accusing the broad of all sorts of things — She pleaded with him that she was a good girl — He wouldn't believe it — Son of a — -locked her up in the hoosegow for the night!" Amazing — — astounding — downright peculiar.

Before long, I'll bet my left shoe, they'll prohibit soldiers to go to Mexico entirely — This place and neighborhood is going to be closed up tighter than a drum as far as "fast women" are concerned — Almost as bad as Miami, Florida — And, sister, that place is closed down!

At present, I'm seated in Battalion Headquarters — I'll sleep here — Of all nights to spend in — Saturday !! damn!! — Its warm here — quiet — The sergeant of the guard is writing up the guard report. — Let me introduce him to you — Sergeant Passmore, bald, stern, wrinkled — age — ah — say forty five. — He silently chews some strange Mexican concoction similar to our chewing gum — His facial muscles, firm and hard, bulge at each bite —

Each line in his face depicts the years of hardships — of torturous experiences. — Four years in the marines — fought in every major battle in the last war — Possessor of the purple heart — There's a man that can truly say "Listen, buck, you're talking to a man who's been around!!"...

Speaking of sergeants in general we might consider, in passing, my motor sergeant — The one who's going to save my face in this motor officer business — Its not so much his physical make-up that I wish to discuss — merely his name — I know it'll cause you to squeal with something or other — — "Trulove" — that's his name — pronounced "True love" — — the thing that gripes me is that every time I get near him I think in terms of true love — and my thoughts turn to the "gal I love" — I guess I'll have to keep away from the motor pool and motor sergeant. — Bad enough to have you haunt my dreams but to have you make me walk around glassy-eyed during the daytime — is too much!!!! — (kiddin'!)

Life goes drearily on and on — Training, training. This gunner's exam is driving me nuts! — Next week there'll be the experts exam and then the men are going on the rifle range — our mobilization program will continue through January and a bit into February — ...

Friday night I visited Lieutenant Buckner in his home…He tried to be hospitable and force scotch and soda down my objecting throat — All I wanted was some of his delicious apples. — We compromised — a little apple — a little whiskey! — And sister when that apple began fermenting or getting drunk on that whiskey — the battle of Dunkirk had nothing on my stomach…

I'll close now, with all my love— …I love you — Sweetheart.

Your
Sid

Dec. 14

Hello darling! —

Let us "tear" ourselves away from the beauties of Fort Bliss and turn our attention for a brief moment to the desert surrounding the camp. Carefully scanning this barren wasteland covered with an endless "Coney Island" we are astounded by the vast expanse of loneliness that strikes us — But wait!! What is that over in the north??? — A cloud of dust! — A grunting groaning engine! — gnashing smashing grinding gears! — We follow the cloud! —

First it goes forward! Then backwards! Squeaks to a stop — roars to a start — stops! races! rears! bucks! snorts!! — Yes, as we'd suspected, it is our little hero, the pitiful soldier — our sorrowful figure learning how to drive a G.P. (General Purpose) — pronounced jeep!

This "learning," as we might call it takes place after hours — from 5:30 until 6:30 P.M. — My instructor is Sergeant Trulove — I'm no whiz at it I'll grant you that — but I made the darn thing go and stop. —By special permission of the Battalion motor officer I've been allotted the same amount of gas allowed for the instruction of new drivers — 43 gallons — with these 43 gallons I intend to work my way up from a jeep to a 2 1/2 ton truck — I hope. Then — following this ambitious program I'll try for a government license! — By the way I wrangled my way out of signing shipping tickets for the motor pool. The new supply officer will take care of that….

Everything's a mass of confusion. Here, the officers are supposed to be giving the men the gunners examination. At their company areas somebody is supposed to be giving the men instruction for the expert exam which comes next week. Also these same officers are instructed to take the exam themselves before Wednesday — I've completed half my gunners exam — doing very nicely thank you! I ought to make first class gunner and then there's the expert exam to follow — Combined with these duties are those of executive officer of a platoon…Thank God for good non-commissioned officers!! — It is truly spoken — The non-coms are the backbone of the army's leadership!

After going off duty Sunday afternoon (officer of the day tour) I stopped by my room showered etc, and hopped into town — dull there — tried Juarez — Even "duller"— came back to town — went to a movie ... — There was included a stage show given by one of Major Bowe's amateur units — interesting!! A quick sandwich and then home. — ...

I'll probably not leave camp for a while — my savings schedule wont allow it — I'll be content with the officers club on post for this weekend — — Let you know what's cooking!!

You <u>are</u> my sweetheart. I <u>do</u> love you. — —

> Your
>
> Sid
>
> —always

Dec. 17

Glory — Glory be!! — — Sweet!! — —congratulations and all the customary bowing that goes with a junior phi beta kappa appointment — What I'd really like to do is just look you in the eye, shrug my shoulders, and boastfully exclaim — Heck — that's what my gal 'Stelle can always do!! — a phi beta in everything!! And that's no lie!! — to put it in army jargon — you're a master gunner — an expert — — — my gentleman!! — my sweet! — my — — anything and everything!! — I'm very happy for you — As a matter of fact I'm elated — for myself !!! — — why? I don't know! — I just tingle with pride — and admiration!! — Good work!!! —

Enough of this praise and coddling — you'll probably get a swelled head and be more difficult than ever to manage (if that were possible!!)

My motor sergeant seems to think I can drive sufficiently well. At least he hasn't given me any driving instruction for the past 2 days — The cad has gone gallavantin' — You see the lessons were given during his free time — Oh well — My problem???

Speaking of problems listen to this choice bit — I've got but two good motor mechanics — one is being transferred to Alabama — the other is going on furlough. For twelve days my 18 vehicles are going to be practically without repair facilities — I dread the next few days —

Expert exam starts tomorrow — ho-hum — more hours of doing nothing — tsk. I'm afraid I'm developing into a regular fiend! I pull surprise spot inspections — one day I inspected the mess kits of all the first platoon — Next I'd spot inspect one of my trucks — lubrication, water, tires, fire extinguisher, equipment, etc. — A regular hound!!! Discovered one truck without an accident report card — Gave driver terrible calling down — frightened myself while doing it!

No I haven't gone into town recently — El Paso holds no attractions for a man not "on the make" —As for Juarez — strictly a tourist town which makes a business of being Mexican — also holds no attraction for a phlegmatic settled jerk!! — The officers' club offers nothing but drinking yourself silly — and I'm silly enough as is — I know — I need a hobby — — but that's you!! — What a horrible existence — heavenly because of you — boring without you (and please refrain from cracks!!) ...

I'll let you in on a little secret — I've had some gifts hanging around my dungeon for two weeks — just too dilatory to send them — The only thing holding me back is my dissatisfaction with the gift I selected for you — — Heck — you always present this problem to me — No — don't tell me — If I can't get anything better you'll just have to be satisfied with the one I send!! —Oh — fiddle faddle — And it probably won't arrive till way after Christmas — more fiddle faddle —

Sweetheart — look, don't ever worry about my worrying (??) about your letters — I'll write as often as humanly possible — you'll write — well — as often as you can — I'm pretty certain! — True — the long silence came after a scolding letter. Hence I found myself uncomfortably close to thinking my goose had been cooked — I imagine it was for a time — but — well — — a cooked goose tastes better anyway — If that makes sense??

Let's see — have I really become that man you spoke about — well — I talk a lot less than previously — I worry a great deal less about unessentials — — Think a great many things I've done and planned to do — childish and immature — Don't go out of my way to make friends — I've got a reputation of being "G.I. Diamond!" — Play the game according to the books — insist on absolute attention to duty! — Like to be told what to do and then not be bothered until I've completed the task — Can't stand men coming to attention as I come into a room — abhor saluting men all the time!! — There you have the present Sidney Diamond — There are definite traces of still existent sense of humor — It'd almost become a vestigial trait — I think motion pictures dull and unappealing. Stay in — every night during the week to write letters, loaf — — Oh — well — — — I'm still

Your
Sid

Dec. 18
My darling! —

Look at me!! Am I so old and unattractive!!!?? Do I look repulsive!!?? — Have I really got that angelic face you mention??? — Am I a prude?

An introverted confirmed "goody" — Don't get frightened — allow me to explain the circumstances —

I was seated in the supply room busily typing some important tables for the exam when in walks my platoon sergeant — Welch —

"Don't think I'm getting personal, lieutenant, but are you single?"

"Yes — sure!!"

"Well, ah, — — er — do you have a date for Christmas Eve"

"Why — er — nope!"

"Well our platoon would like to give a party in town with girls and all!"

"Fine — what can I do for you??"

"Well, ——-sir—Would you come — as –er—ah sort of—<u>chaperon</u>!!! (???***+x+)

Chaperon!! — me — Sidney Diamond — so good so noble — on equal terms with the old maids of yester year — — I'd tried to get these men to respect me, of course, but when respect goes so far as to ask me to protect the "honor" of a load of El Paso "dames" well!!! — I could just see them saying to their girl friends —

"Don't worry it'll be a nice party — besides we have our lieutenant there as <u>chaperon</u>" — ugh — and again ugh —

I gave them the only possible answer —

"Of course, I'll be only too glad to oblige — but remember I'm a strict and diligent officer" — —

Fortunately for my pride, or is it ego, they couldn't get the sanction of the company commander, who, like most men, is afraid to assume unnecessary responsibilities — hence no party — so far — thank God!!!...

There isn't much else to discuss — oh yes my adventure in the desert this evening — Tonight — my third lesson in jeep driving and control — My instructor, a bit bored with the routine driving up and down the road decided a trip across the "boondikes" (or something) would do me good — The "boondikes" as they call them consist of soft sandy desert with little clumps of bushes on top of small mounds of sand closely covering the land. After getting stuck three times I finally got the hang of it and went tearing across these bumps like a madman — — bumped and slid — bounced — veered — backed — growled — groaned — — We were thrown in every direction — I spent more time out of my seat than in! ...

I still need some polish — a lot of shining — I can make a good jeep busting jeep cowboy but lack the finesse of a driver —

Sweetheart — oh well — look don't kill yourself trying to get mail to me Just drop a short note once in awhile — — let me know you're not angry — that the situation's normal!! That's all I need — tell me your worries, your cares — — share them with me if you find it difficult to get others to comfortably listen—— write me — I'd enjoy it — — Show me you still care enough to be willing to pour out your troubles — —

What troubles??? — I don't know?? — — just in case you have some — — or something —

<u>Statement of fact — I love you</u> — — —

Your
Sid

The excitement of new places and responsibilities was giving way to loneliness.

December 27, 1942

Hello sweet!! — a sad sorry situation — I haven't written in God-knows-how-long. — Maybe it's this "wild" Christmas activity or something — I really couldn't say! — I'll try and gather up the loose threads of the relatively dull and uninteresting life of the "Nuts and Bolts King" (as you would have it!) — Let's see — I wrote Christmas day but again tore the letter up — (Horrible waste of energy — what??) — So that would leave Christmas eve and following!! — okay — in the usual event by event manner — I proceed!! TA-DAH-DAH!!

Christmas eve — wandered into town alone — over to Mexico for a Mexican supper — drink — back to El Paso — movie — Burgess Meredith in <u>Street of Chance-</u> action — drama — continuous suspense and puzzle — surprise ending — Still alone — still wandering — I went into the Cortez Hotel — asked if there was a dance anywhere in town — They directed me to the 10th floor ballroom — Walked in on some Mexican club "night of memories" — It was fascinating to watch some of the Mexican jitterbug or something — fortunately for this adventurous youth he knew the singer of the band. Possibly as a result of her being drunk — but I mean stewed! — Possibly as a result of my good looks (I doubt that) anyway — she greeted me like a long lost cousin — We danced a bit and then I had to leave in order to get back to camp by curfew hour — 2 A.M....

Christmas day — warm — sunny — almost perspiring —...I went to my company area for the company Christmas dinner — (the menu will follow by subsequent post) — It was really a swell affair — All the other officers brought their wives and children — we had the colonel as our guest — and his family — Some of the men brought their friends — Everything was bedecked with Christmas finery — We had a large Christmas tree — The most memorable event of the meal was one of the children crying — I hadn't heard something like that for ages!! — To get on with this odyssey—From there I went into Juarez — witnessed a bull-fight — Conecirito fought. He's that dashing matador I spoke to you about a while ago — ...

Oh well — we find ourselves back in town — oh yes — I went to a synagogue — the only one in town — — to pray?? — I doubt it — To find some people who reminded me of home — perhaps?? — To waste an evening — Probably!! Synagogue large — congregation very small — ...After the service they had a sort of community discussion — All the young bucks home from college for Christmas were on the pulpit — discussing the influence of the war on college curricula — a familiar topic no doubt! — Was introduced around to the people....

Saturday — a dress parade in the A.M. — then a lecture by Major Woodwill — hero of world war number one — ...

In the afternoon some routine administrative duties — then I went to town — that was last night — Left for town early — haircut — uniform pressed — supper — then I met Alice — who's Alice?? — well — she's half Mexican, half Scotch — dark-haired — not too good looking — has a few Indian features about her — we went to the officers club where we had a long and lengthy talk about Mexico and Mexicans — Her stories about mediums and ghosts which she swore were true — Visits fortune-tellers every few weeks — believes one of them faithfully — oh well — home again — another long trolley ride — sleep — now!!!

Sweetheart—I know I've been running around like a chicken with its throat cut — Every time I go out its sort of a search — a longing — Perhaps you feel similarly — I don't know — Something to fill the emptiness — Movies are very good — Well –I know I love you — I know now that I can't remain aloof to it — that I can't feel indifferent about what happens to our love — I feel so uncivilized — just wanting you — and caring naught for worldly practicalities — For something I brought on myself its not bad — but not good —... You needn't wax sarcastic either — I do love you — so there — nothing can possibly change my mind — not even you!

Sweet —

Your dulce corazon

Sid

Dec. 29

My sweet —

All is serene — the hyper-tension of the week-end is gone — the usual calm, collected, stolid Sid is back to normalcy — back to the nuts, the bolts, the endless checking — endless supervision — interminable reading of military pamphlets and such junk!! — The usual evening "coke" is there before me — Your picture back over my left shoulder amongst the shoe-shining kits, shampoos, and hats — — The mind, what little of it remains for disorganized non- "G.I." thinking, stealthily crawls towards thoughts of home and you — — — Peculiar how useless and vain has been my Christmas week attempt to arrange a new life in El Paso — It can't be done — not as long as there is a tie as strong as my affection for you....

How are my pretty little jacket and thunderbird (or haven't they arrived yet) — You can get it changed if you don't like the fit — I drove that store half-mad with my explanation of what you looked like They asked "how much she weighed?" — I won't tell — might have over-estimated — and why kill true love with a mere ten pounds or so. — "How tall?" — There were six salesgirls in the store and I had each one try it on — Each underwent a close scrutiny for size, shape, and hips, shoulders, and "other dimensions" — The thing which really drove me crazy was choosing a suitable color — yoiks!! — it was disgusting — Red — nah she's the quiet type — Blue — well I want a little color — I know the white'll get dirty more easily. But what the heck — physics will prove that white is nothing more than a combination of all the basic colors so-oo-oo—logical??? — no? — so I'm not so brilliant !!

Let's see — ah yes — yesterday, Sunday — what'd I do — after writing you that lengthy monstrosity I settled down to some solid doing nothing — Just visited my company area — took care of a few minor details and then went to the Fort Bliss officers' club for dinner — There was a dance going on — Jimmy Fields and his orchestra — Not having a gal — and not being the kind to bust in on someone else's evening (I know how I felt when it was done to me!) — I retired to the reading room — wrapped myself up in a soft chair — a copy of the "Infantry Journal" — and a rum-coke with added lime — then home and sleep — tossed a bit — thought of you — called myself a dumb fool twice said you were wonderful four times — then said "nuts" and went off to meet morpheus.

As usual my roommate and his visitor Lieutenant Millard are discussing women — They think I'm cracked!! — so what!! — what the devil — I love you — period — keep me posted on the home front status —...

I have resigned myself to my fate of being hopelessly and irrevocably in love — in love with you —

Your

Sid

On December 29, the very day that the previous letter was written, I received the Christmas presents Sid had sent—a beautiful woven wool jacket from New Mexico and a Thunderbird pin.

PART 2: 1943

As the new year began, I was busy with school and friends, and although I loved Sid, I was afraid of what the physical distance between us would do to our relationship. Sid remained steadfast. ("L.F.D." stood for Little Fickle Dame.)

Jan. 6

Hello my sweet —

...Sweetheart, I love you—you know how much I want to be with you and near you—you know how much I respect and adore you. Well——look—I'm absolutely a total flop at pretending—I'll manage to have good times and that sort of tommy-rot but don't ask me to pretend I made no "vows" or promises — and, look, if you really want me to feel that you're "only the girl I happen to love at the moment and who happens to love me" — frankly, I'm entirely stumped! — You say "Won't it be better that way!" —— My darling — I could go for years perhaps with a hundred different girls and never would I become "confused," or the least bit swayed from you and my wishes as far as you're concerned.

I know you're an L.F.D. — old or new — but you <u>are</u> a "gentleman" — and don't say otherwise!!...

Am I dreaming up "windmills" again or are you attempting to be "noble"—If it's the latter I'll never forgive you for being so lacking in the basic knowledge of Sid!!—Remember — we were to play this game as one gentleman to another — whatever's griping our relationship ought to be brought forth for close examination — my only comment about the whole affair is (as my men would say) Well I'll be a sad sack!!!!

I love you.

Your

Sid

Jan. 14

Hello my darling —

...I've been working on my new pair of shoes for the last hour and a half. First saddle soap, then dry — then oil — then polish. This, all to make the leather soft, pliable, endurable and assist in weather-proofing. Also to prevent the leather from cracking as a result of this dry weather. These shoes are more important than any of the other more expensive pairs I have. A size too large to allow for spread of the feet on long marches and to permit the wearing of two or three pairs of socks during the cold of winter — whenever I come across such a climate — Carefully worked

[on] for days before the initial wearing of the shoes — This should answer all the field requirements.

The weather is again griping! — Extremely cold nights and mornings which cause one to wear an overcoat — and burning hot in the noon so that one is tempted to remove even one's shirt! This continuous outrageous behavior of the weather has caused me to look forward to the six days on the range Jan. 28-Feb. 6 with no little apprehension, — We will be living in tents...

"My" trucks are being neglected because of this practice in rifle marksmanship — oh worry, worry — Like love these machines must be nurtured by a diet of constant attention, by proper food for the soul. If not, they grow rusty, balky, cranky! They are more difficult to maneuver and control. If left without care for a sufficient length of time they just wilt. They no longer respond to their drivers!! Love, like automobiles, must be oiled, gassed, and continually nursed. The lubrication is most important of all. For without this necessary factor the rough spots clash and extreme friction and heat develop — then — goodbye truck! Goodbye love!! — Let's always remember to "lubricate"! —

> I love you
> Your
> Sid

Jan. 15
Sweetheart —

Firm, stoic young miss — Hard and unyielding. What strong violent adjectives for one such as thou! As I've said a thousandfold times whatever cometh forth from thy lips shall be my law! So "we" become brave idiots for the duration plus six months, strong and courageous; no wimpering, no sadness, no sorrows, just you and me(?) and an understanding! Frankly, reading your letters amazes me each time. You're always on your toes when you read letters from Estelle — ah yes. —

She'll burn you with the inanities of love. Freeze you with scornful rebukes, tickle you with quiet humor. Anger you with paradoxical inconsistencies. On one hand kind and understanding. On the other harsh and stubborn — Probably something she eats!! — — But with it all — her beauty — her grace — her comradeship — add up to the most wholesome character in existence. Perhaps I speak with the tongue of the "lover" etc, but these are the facts and I've seldom been a bearer of tales!...

Daily routine continues along the uneventful, dull track it chose at the beginning. Now the men are going in for practice and more practice in rifle marksmanship. I'm here again, Room 37, pipe, coke, and wind playing violent weird rhythms around the corners of the building. It hasn't blown this way in a month. Sand all over the place. In every crevice, every opening, crack, ears, nostrils, mouth — In the day time one can see the oncoming sand — Like a huge ball of wool it rolls across the desert and finally envelops you in its maelstrom of grit and discomfiture!

I'm going to try to get a call to you tonight. — You needn't worry about the bill. By merely saying, "charge it to my bill at the officer's mess" I can sit here calmly writing to you while the two or three hours go by getting the call through to New York.

> I love you —
> Your
> Sid

Jan. 16

My darling,

What's the use — First you write in a peculiar manner common only to womankind which makes a man feel like a darn fool for whispering words of love and affection. Then there's a green light signal which says "go ahead — If its true — I want to hear it!" — There's absolutely no known means of making you happy so I'll just have to maintain a strict adherance to the policy of truth — and pour out slush that seems to eat my very insides — to tell you of the strange emptiness — of the loneliness for you. — Ah yes, I forgot — "Go hungry, pet — good and hungry!" — you said — — Well — these are the unadulterated facts — even with the risk of having them returned in an unsavory manner — —I love you, want you, dream of you — think of you constantly. Sweetheart, I'm happy! I work a full 8 hours or so from 8 until 5:30 — go home to my barracks, read, talk, maybe study Spanish. Why darling I'm more faithful than most of the married men around this place. On the week-ends — Well I just get the "oige" to do something which will get me away from hup! hoop! hep! haw! And constant stiff-backed firmness. Don't ever fear my even thinking of another. Why when I do go out with someone else I only talk of my girl back home!! — impolite, I know, but I love you so hopelessly.... I think you're tops— ...

> Your
> Sid

59

Jan. 22

My darling —

Let's look about this room, this desk of simple design and practical construction put together hastily. Its top is covered with the rubbish of male-kind. On the left, an unsmoked cigar jutting out from between a "Time" magazine and an "American Mercury" — beneath them is (TM405) The Army Cook and [?] Company Administration. This is the side belonging to my roommate. A bottle of lighter fluid, empty! A small compact traveller's alarm clock and, for some odd reason, a regular silver dining room knife complete the area used by him.

On the right we find Lt. Diamond's equipment — stacked high is an imposing column of unread books. "Reading I've Liked" by you-know-who, (FM 25-10) "Motor Transport," (TM 21-300) "Driver Selection and Training" and a Soldier's Handbook comprise his right-hand library. — a bottle of ink next — then a clothes brush and bottle of lighter fluid, full! A copy of (FM7-10) "Rifle Company Rifle Regiment" comes next. In the center and ready for immediate action are his counter-bug materiel. Some Vicks' vaporub for the nostrils, Listerine for the sore throat and aspirins because his mother always gave them to him when he felt ill. Quite an imposing lot. His alarm clock is on the floor close to his bed so that it may be turned off more quickly and slumber resumed!! This desk is situated before the one window we have. We have little trouble opening or closing it because attempts to do so are unnecessary. The wind finds its way through the walls and cracks and infiltrates through the room regardless of how tightly the window is shut. The sand and dust could seemingly get into a hermetically vacuum-packed can let alone be stopped by mere boards!! From the window may be seen the lights on the roads leading to El Paso. Occasionally the mournful wail of a passing troop train and its clacking wheels pounding "Praise the Lord!"

This could go on for days but detailed descriptions are the things which are usually very hastily scanned, if not completely ignored! It brings to mind the lengthy heart-to-heart talk I had with one of my men this afternoon. His wife seemed to have forgotten the essential billing and cooing which is what "makes" the average letter. But—let me explain more thoroughly.

It seems this man had been in continual hot water. Arguments with his non-coms, several tours of company punishment, an almost court martial...After I'd given the men a lecture on Emergency Relief for soldiers families etc. he came up to me...Here's his story. It might just as well be that of hundreds of others.

"Lieutenant Diamond, sir, I can't think straight. It's my wife, sir. I love her so much — she's on my mind all day, sir — — I really don't mean to be bad, I just don't realize what I'm doing! You see we were seperated for awhile just 'afore I joined the army. I'm a jealous cuss — can't stand to have another man even look at her — That's why she left me — I know she won't have no truck with anyone else but I just can't drive her outta my head." — ...

[I said:] "I suggest you get your wife out of your system.... The only way it can be done is by good hard work...Honest-to-goodness effort in becoming a good soldier will help a good deal....I'm not married but there's a girl back home I hope to marry when this mess is over. I'm fairly certain she'll be there when I come back — ...Period! be satisfied, be confident in your wife's love and go into your present job with all the vitality you can muster— "

Ah., the problems of the young junior officer....

This has been a long boring epistle, I know, but you'll recall that I'd always said that one of the disadvantages to our relationship was that you'd have to listen to my glib prattlings for hours on end — and when tired you'd say "enough!!" I don't know, darling, why I couldn't just fill up a letter with gush of a page or two and quit. But somehow when I write to you I feel like a child talking to his sister or mother — pouring out his endless drone of daily incidents — boring her with his repetitious tales — But she only smiles warmly and urges him to continue on! — You're such a swell individual — I'm proud to be your friend — Even more proud that you seem to rate me so high. My sweet, my darling, my love.

Your

Sid

Jan. 25

My darling!—

...Darling you seem to be interested in my happiness — try not to be too worried about my welfare — I can't tolerate your being so lonely for me. Its not right, its not fair — Darling — I don't know what exactly to say — If I say, "make a new life for yourself" you'll get angry and misinterpret — Just toss the old boy out of your mind — Say he's not worth it (and that's putting it mildly!) We can't have the best part of this combination feeling blue. Me, I'm okay! Lonely for you? Yes, but heck kid that's no reason for you to worry and fret. — There I go, trying to be 'noble' or something — I might as well face the facts. I love you, I love you overwhelmingly. I do care a great deal whether or not you still feel the same way about me but darling — this thing's going on for a long while — let's face it as two who are firm in their love for each other. Save me somewhere in a corner of your mind and when I come home we can oil it up, take [off] the rust, dust it off and we'll run 'er the same as always. Mean-time put the old boiler in storage — Chalk it up to rationing — including affection! — It'll all come back in the future — I'm certain — and I want you to be certain!!!

I love you, love you, love you

Your
Sid

In the course of a long letter in February, he expressed his love of country, described what he saw, and shared with me his thoughts as he headed toward the Dona Anna Range for rifle practice.

...My love for country as you put it is basic — its love for a way of living — its affection not for inane expressions such as "liberty" and "Democracy"— It's a deep urge crying out that such and such is wrong — It is cruel — It is even more selfish and bestial than what exists at home — that it must be eliminated if ever home can be improved!

Perhaps if I told you of this morning — perhaps if I tried by revolting man-made words to describe the thoughts that swished through my mind you might get an inkling of how I feel —

As is usual, now, we left early in the morning. Darkness still kissed the earth...We were once more headed towards Don Anna Range.

Before me was the red twinkling light of the jeep carrying the company commander. The three heads bobbed up against the skyline in a manner similar to the turkey's wobbling head. To the rear stretched for a seemingly infinite space could be observed the gentle twinkle of the headlights of the lumbering two and one half ton trucks. There was nothing to do but meditate — and look about—...

On our right, in the east, the sun dazzled the clouds with its golden brilliance. The clouds in turn blinked and reflected the light on to each other.— Like God's childish smudges in the sky these clouds hung in perfect lack of symmetry. Outlined against the horizon in deep purple hues the Huego mountain chain reached for the skies. I imagined one sitting on the top of those peaks and saying "hyah" to passing angels.

A hawk jumped from a telephone pole and swooped down amongst the mounds in search of prey.

To my left stood the Franklin Mountains illuminated by heaven's neon lights—a pink purple mixture. Each nook and cranny accentuated by its shadow.

Believe me if I tell you that the jeep's motor became an organ and a choir of a thousand voices singing surging heart-stirring music...

My driver, from upper New York State muttered—"I ain't seen nuthin' like this in my whole life!" A jack- rabbit jumped in front of our headlights—looked at us a moment with big frightened eyes and then scurried away—

The wind was still—It had gone for this morning. The air had a supernatural warmth about it. I knew we were trespassing on forbidden property — No worldly human could be allowed to share such splendor...

A strange unique sense of freedom—of thankfulness for living, for having lived—of joy in the richness of my life—its fullness—crawled through me. I slouched down in the uncomfortable jeep and cuddled up with myself—"Yep!" — I mused —"I got no kicks!"...

Let's come down to the more down to earth facts — ...Today our men did some combat firing — that is they'd simulate an attack by the enemy with an exchange of blank ammunition. Then we'd hide some targets in the underbrush and give them some live ammunition to fire at the targets as they advanced, to test their accuracy of fire under battle conditions.

'Stelle, I must have gained ten years on my life worrying about whether or not they'd shoot each other. I almost feinted while I watched one man take deliberate aim over the head of another on the verge of rising to move forward —— I was either too stunned to shout a warning or afraid to yell for fear I'd startle the soldier, he might let go his round carelessly. — I sighed a heavy sigh of relief when he finally did fire and the bullet sped over the prostrate soldier — about four feet above him! — (an officer is always responsible for the safety of his men — he can never delegate that responsibility). Oh- yes — There's been a shake-up in the battalion and our company has two new officers. Because I know the men I've been put in charge of my platoon with the new officer who outranks me as second in command. — ...

Please excuse any lack of regularity in letters — we're going in for extremely intensive testing of men and units in the next few weeks. So please, please, please — don't start reading between lines — Don't, don't, don't think of my changing —— please?? — If I wander a short distance, a very short distance — remember I'm away, alone, — too young or too goody-goody to associate with the older officers — too eccentric to find enjoyment in drowning my sorrows — and too impatient to indulge in lengthy discussions of women! — ...

Please know that whatever I do—whatever may happen—I'll never change as far as you're concerned—I can't—You're a part of me—I belong to you—If I sometimes act like a cranky baby chalk it up to a lack of sleep!...Remember, as I always try to — one hundred and fourty men will depend on my decisions. They will live or die as a result of my thoughts....This new sense of responsibility has grown within me during the past few months — ...

Sometimes I envy those who can just sit about and tend to their own particular job and forget that there are others — — You've got to sweat with your men — cry with the anger of fatigue — curse — yell — before you can appreciate how much you fear for their well-being.—

Be sure of me sweetheart—always be sure of me —

Your
Sid

In a letter of Feb. 26, Sid defended his having enlisted against all the advice of family and friends, comparing his resolve to the stubbornness in a just cause of the main character in Ibsen's An Enemy of the People. He also made a passionate plea in defense of those often thought of as "the common herd." "This herd can be taught, must be taught — It is the duty of those who see, to help them, not to cast them down as ignorant, stupid — They can think — They can struggle — They are doing just that — "

In March, the battalion was moved to Shreveport, Louisiana for further training

Darling,

Thirty-seven hours the troops have been journeying—many more hours still face them. They'd been expecting this move for weeks. Rumors...had been flourishing amongst them for endless days and nights. Few trusted their ears. They had the soldier's philosophy of believing only when seeing. For a week prior the preparations increased at fever pitch. Clearances were obtained. Personal affairs attended to. Insurance policies arranged for. Wives sent home. Good-byes to Mexican sweethearts made. A last Saturday night spree in Juarez and then the inevitable wait!—The waiting that is such a gnawing factor in all army movements.

First the wait for induction. The wait for rail movements. The wait for embarkation orders. The horrible frightening wait for battle!

All the bedding had been turned in. The trucks had been loaded on flat cars. The men slept on the floor. A few buildings down light still emanated from the orderly room. The officers were there, worrying—Yes, frightfully afraid of overlooking some detail. Had they enough food? Ice?

Would a man be released from the hospital and cause confusion? Could we maintain control over men during stops? Had we made the safety precautions clear?…

The ceaseless activity in anticipation of the move now degenerated into that nervous impatience for the train to go!

At a very early hour in the morning the stillness of the dark was blasted by the shriek of a sergeant's whistle! One could sense the anxious curiosity of the men. Blankets quickly rolled; packs hastily slung; equipment adjusted. They were ready!

A roll call by the light of a flashlight. What, a man missing!! No, no he'd just been asleep on his feet. He hadn't heard his name.

Silently the column moved through the fort…

After arrival at the railroad siding they waited some more. Waited in the black darkness—interested in the movements of the train people making up the train. They'd bring a few Pullman cars, maneuver them over twisting turns, then bring up the flat cars with the trucks…a long train was born.—The noise of the banging and clashing of the cars was all that broke the quiet!—

Roll call and assignment of men to their berths and all was ready. The guards made a hasty check of the truck fastenings then took their position in the caboose…

From somewhere along train route — past San Antonio — been traveling 33 hrs.

Hiya — Travel like a King or prince at least! Private compartment all for this lowly lieutenant — my own wash stand, hot and cold running water, a chair and two cushioned seats to lounge on. — ice water — an electric fan — heat — private toilet — yoiks! I could travel this way for days!!

The country is improving the further east we go. Saw the first honest-to-goodness tree I'd seen in 3 months. There is also some vegetation pleasant to look at. And the sight of black fertile soil astounds me! The green of the countryside soothes the eye!!   Our trip has been entirely pleasant so far. Everything went off smoothly….

Sid

March 11
My darling! —

Louisiana, at long last! — Trees!! — glorious green trees!! — tall ones, green foliage — a bed of pine needles — streams!! — stinking mud-holes!

Torrential rain but its heaven. Like children we never could appreciate candy when we had too much of it. Hence our dislike for the sun! —

The humidity is high almost comparable to Edgewood.

Yoiks there's so much to write about. So much I want to say, to record for you to share with me, and I must get it off at once because the lord only knows how much time I'll have in the future to write....

We left Fort Bliss before breakfast Monday morning. The men ate from paper plates all the way down. They'd file back to the kitchen car (which was nothing more than a baggage car fitted with field ranges and an ice-box) and be served their meals. Then move back to the pullman to eat.

Its strange how large a country we live in. One could travel for hours through Texas without seeing a soul. To bother mentioning the towns would be useless. The further east we moved the more prosperous became the farm houses. No longer were we accosted by the ugly adobe huts made from mud. Here were houses, homes, made from finished wood.

The scenery in Texas was the same. If you've seen a hundred yards of West Texas you've seen all of West Texas. The unwelcoming hard rocky soil or the endless emptiness of the sand-covered "boondocks" which are nothing more than mounds of sand surrounding the ever present mesquite bush. The barrel cactus, the yucca rod, the greasewood bush, the prickly pear all made-up the desert. The occasional rabbit scampering across our path and the howl of the coyote....

As we came to East Texas the terrain gradually improved. From the endless miles of wasteland and shaggy mountains we came to more pleasant rolling country. Trees grew larger the further along the road we traveled. First the scrawny ugly mesquite then the tall stately pines. We came upon farmland. Endless joyous miles of fertile black soil. This black was even more accentuated because the earth had been turned over in preparation for spring planting. Row upon row of neat lines of "Good Earth." Sometimes the lines running away from the railroad would be broken by another plowed area running perpendicular to it. We arrived in Shreveport at 12 P.M. — Saw nothing of this town. I was officer of the day (the only one awake). I met the new train- conductor who had the secret orders for our next move. That's the way troop trains travel. The train crew never knows where we're going. Every day or stop we'd pick up a new train conductor who'd direct us on the next phase of the trip. After the train had been serviced we started out again. Travelled all night and finally were instructed to unload at a siding in the middle of nowhere.

We're located now somewhere near Leesville.

At present we're just marking time — just getting used to this sort of life —

Bivouaced in a pine-tree forest. Intriguing country. We've had nothing but rain since we arrived. — a pleasant change — a little to much though

Strange how much I thought of us on that long journey. As we came into our present area Weiner (a boy from N.Y.) remarked — "Just like Prospect Park eh? — or Central Park!" — I almost choked from the pangs of pleasing memories. No 59th St. Station or Bloomingdale's here — but I can dream can't I—

"And thou, beside me, singing in the Wilderness
Ah Wilderness, were Paradise enow!"

Now I really have it bad.

> I love you.
> Your
> Sid

March 15
I love you — ...

A few days ago I went on a reconnaissance through the neighboring country roads. In between noting the tenths of miles on the speedometer, following the map, and holding on for dear life (my jeep driver is a frustrated tank driver — so help me!) I caught glimpses of the lumber country of Louisiana and East Texas. We traveled for miles and miles through the interminable forests of pines. Suddenly out of the green wall of trees we'd be accosted by a small clearing. A house, a barn, a cow or two and then we'd be back in the woods again.

Strange about these houses deep in the wilderness. They all needed a painting. All looked as if ages had passed on since they'd been constructed. One had an old man on the porch who waved to us as we rode by. Many were surrounded by pink blossomed peach trees....

Here we'd see a farmer clearing land. Clearing a forest of trees so that he may plant some more food the next year. The back-breaking toil as the tree is chopped down. He grunts as each strong stroke of the axe pecks away at the bleeding tree. Nearby a young 'un works on an already fallen tree. He cleans off the branches and takes them to a scrap heap where they are burned. We see the smoke arising from a still-burning stump. They burn the stump down to the ground....

I love you —

To describe the emotions of one Sid Diamond as he sits here before his tent with the wind shuffling through the trees and the sun twinkling between the branches would be hopeless. His thoughts are clear. His dreams are clear. They all encompass 'Stelle — 'Stelle — the epitome of female-kind — Once more to hold her in my arms. Once more to smother her with kisses. Once more to laugh at the theatre — to argue at prices. Once again to talk freely and frankly with my love — Heaven grant me that! —

> Your
> Sid

March 16

My sweet! —

It is evening. My flashlight dully illuminates the page. Someone crackles the leaves outside my tent. A sergeant curses out one of his squad. The platoon headquarters men argue about women. A cricket makes noises. A soldier shouts — "I can't take it — early to bed and early to rise."...We are settling into night.

Above, the dark rain-soaked clouds race across the leaves. They'll burst again sometime during the evening. Tomorrow, again, everything will be damp. Tomorrow in the hush of the morning, even before the dew has come I'll hear that shy voice "Lt. Diamond, Lieutenant — 5:15 — 5:15 sir!" — Then I'll fumble for my clothes and tumble out to take the morning report.

Breakfast at 6:00 A.M. Then a trip to the cassock outpost guarding a field suspected as a possible landing place for parachute troops.

The insects seem to be calling to each other now — I'm weary — desperately in love — I feel in the mood to lean on your shoulder — to close my eyes — to drowse — sleep. Even to talk to you, under this spell, — of silly idiotic things — store windows — santa claus — anything —

...Burning your bridges are you? — don't! — Remember the most basic rule of selection of position. — Always choose an <u>alternate position</u> in case this one becomes useless. The alternate position is one which, although situated differently, can accomplish the same mission. And the <u>mission</u> we are <u>both</u> concerned with is <u>your happiness!</u> Darling I suggest a rereading of the "Rubaiyat of Omar Kayam" with a fuller understanding of our present situation — Don't fret about misunderstanding — I'll love you — always — So enjoy life while you still can.

> Your
> Sid

I wanted so much to be <u>with</u> Sid that I even imagined sharing his experiences. He had to disabuse me of such fantasies.

March 28

Hello Sweet —

The "war," as we call each phase of maneuver, is over. Once more one can sit in comparative ease and think of home and people surrounding such memories. Ten days of hell have just passed. Ten days of anxiety, of sweat, of mud, of torture, yes — even starvation for a day or so —

The last communication I received speaks of your desire to share my experiences. A desire to be a part of my experiences.

Will you share my anxious fear as I had my men and mortars cross a river in assault boats? Neither they nor I had ever seen one before. — Had I overloaded the boats? — Could the 400 lb. mortars be lowered down a 20 ft shear drop to the river with no casualties? — How to gather my platoon together in the dark when the boats had landed over the entire opposite shore? —

One cart and mortar got out of hand and went hurtling down the cliff. — nobody hurt — ammunition boxes and men came rolling down in a mad mixture of arms, legs, and boxes. —

Once on the other side there came the long silent night march behind the infantry — The engineers couldn't get the bridge made in time — our trucks couldn't cross and follow us — The kitchen was on the other side — our rations (emergency) became depleted — I noticed the increased irritability of myself as well as my men. — "I thought we had it rough walking with packs but you men with mortars + packs — hm-mm!"

We simulated some protective fire of high explosive shell — fired a smoke screen for an attack that failed. — So it went — day in and day out. — 10 sloppy days — no washing, no clean clothes — weary slobbering along.

Then it rained!!! —

Everything soaking wet — No chance to let things dry — no opportunity to get comfortable — no fires permitted (disclose position to enemy) — Another day without chow — kitchen truck was lost. — Supply truck lost — Endless winding logging trails recorded on no maps. Didn't even show on aerial photos — Maintenance truck put out of action by artillery fire —

Sometimes we stumbled through the mud — on other occasions we'd advance by bounds in beer trucks — Rotten roads — Once a bridge was blown out — the engineers had to make a new road —

To top it all off I had to get a reprimand for not arranging to get a man back to take his syphilis injection on time. No communication to the rear echelon. It was shocking!!

In the middle of the night after much wandering around we found our position. An artillery officer — in tears, had just sat down and said — "God damn it I'm waiting until daylight!"

The last few days our regimental Command post was surrounded — My men gave up the mortars — fought a delaying action as infantrymen while our trucks and mortars escaped — Later my truck drivers had to get out and defend the trucks for themselves. — The cooks picked up rifles — — We fought as rear guard — backing up slowly. Holding as long as we could —

Whole battalions were lost — Companies were wiped out — (all simulated of course) — We caught it from all directions

Conflicting reports came from all directions — five different officers were giving the same number of conflicting orders. Our roads were blocked — At one time I had to commit my platoon into a battle against 2 companies in an attempt to delay them — Held them for twenty minutes and then the umpire instructed us to retreat — "retire!" — We pulled out to their flanks and hid in the woods — We could watch them all go by — a seemingly endless stream —

You still want to share my experiences — How about sharing my one source of pleasure — Every clear night I always look to the heavens — Sentimental cuss!! — Orion the Hunter and the Seven Sisters are my favorites — Find them — look at them — and nine times out of ten you'll know that I also have enjoyed their warmth sometime that evening —

I love you — I do — No — don't think of sharing the ugly parts of my life — It makes me shudder to think of your undergoing the same hell.

> I repeat —
> I love you.
> Your
> Sid

March 31

My darling!

Life goes wearily on and on. We're devoting this rest period to additional training of the men. Camouflage, control, discipline, dispersion, etc. all need special emphasis.

70

We're completely bivouacked near Anococo (somewhere in Louisiana) Sleeping on the ground is not as bad as its groaned up to be! oo—oo—oo.

The only difficulty we have is the swine which continually rove through our camp. This country is sort of free range, particularly after the army men have destroyed the majority of fences and barbed wire enclosures. Cows walk into our midst nonchalantly munching their cud. Hogs invade the tents of sleeping soldiers who've cached some candy in their bag. A goat family scrambles across the road. Dogs run in packs. All dig into the old garbage pits of the former camping spots.

This is the poorest country for farming I've yet encountered. Just one foot of black rich soil then hard red clay.

Horned toads, snakes, chameleons, spiders and so on complete the picture....

Look—These "wars" will recommence shortly—Whatta ya say to being a bit understanding when no mail arrives and just keep on writing. You can't possibly realize the elation a letter from you brings—especially when you're...in a slit trench, shivering, with the water up to your center—okay?

> I love you—
> sincerely—
> Sid
> I love you—

April 10
Darling!—

Tomorrow I'll be all of twenty-one...It'll be Sunday. I doubt whether we'll be moving. I can enjoy the cookies that mom and dad sent as my birthday feast...

When I do hit that twenty-one I'll know that I've done my share, am doing my utmost to become an individual capable of understanding the value of liberty and the importance of maintaining the "eternal vigilance," to jealously guard that heritage of freedoms. Platitudes? Kid stuff?—of course—...

'Stelle, I've grown up—a great deal. No more moonstruck silly kid—I can appreciate what I had—far more than you can possibly conceive. But given the same situation again I wouldn't hesitate to do what I'm certain is the only correct thing!

Me? I'm just a little guy? The only thing I excel in is mediocrity but I feel sure that whatever hardships I undergo or will undergo my opinions, my determination will not be marred!

What brought this on?—I know—the "Halevah" Mother sent. Imagine people who've never heard of Halevah!!—No one here had and all the officers lined up to taste this new delicacy from Russia manufactured in "New York, N.Y., U.S.A."

Oh yes—don't bother with a rebuttal to that spree I had in rhetorical booshwash —

I love you—

Your

Sid

In the following letter, Sid, at first humorously, in an exaggerated "Brooklyn accent," and then more seriously, tried to answer my doubts and fears. (Charles Boyer and Ronald Colman were well-loved movie actors.)

Darling—

Me? I'm tough, see! —I sleeps on de ground. I eats rough "vittles." —nobody gets de better'a me — no sireee — Dere's only one ting whats got me perplex – er – perp – er a —screwy – and dat's a dame—see? Whatta babe—cute?—nothin' better! A looker?—tops! Yeah – and even talks intell – intel – er – a – smart-like! Ya get me? Yeah!! Once she tells me I'm nuts —— dat don't botter me none! She tells me I'm an imbe- –imbec – er – a dope! –

Foist she's sugar, honey and schmaltz – den she gets to naggin and raisin' de roof wid me! She treats me rough and tough – whadda I do?—whadda I do????—I takes it! —takes it wid all de screwy looks 'n ways of Charles Boyer —I suffers like who's dat guy—a—Ronal Coleman! —'o course I ain't as pretty as dat guy—no, I aint got a line, but cripes I'm in love!

I tries to tell her of de sky, de trees, de boids, de scenery.—She tells me I'm childish?.—Smart like a whip, my babe! Uses big woids – ain't "childish" a big woid??-

Sweetheart – joking aside, I love you, love you to the utmost. My darling, listen—if this war takes ten years, yes, even twenty years I'll finish college! For more reasons than one! Did you know I was born under the sign of Aries, the goat – or something —— according to my horoscope, they tell me, I have all the persistency, revolting stupid stubbornness of the goat. A goat would bat his head against a wall until dead—maybe there's something in this horoscope deal huh??

Marry you??:—get us all the things we need??— I will!! —

Darling, let's both thank heavens we both have a healthy sense of humor. My little silk-stocking-selling-saleswoman. —

No, I haven't grown up — not at all — I still blush when people tease me about the "notorious 'Stelle!" — Get flustered like an adolescent school boy —

So I suffer from softening of the brain — that's really getting down to fundamentals! — basic!!

You "want to know where we stand in my estimation" —

I can only speak for myself. I know I love you. I know things have not changed as far as I'm concerned. — A little dubious, perhaps, about fitting into to the scheme of civilian living when this is over — but I imagine I'll get into the swing of things after a few weeks — a trifle worried about being teased about this deal for the rest of our blissful (and it will be happy) lives — Regardless of how you think — please respect my right to believe in certain stupidities —

Sure, I'm a dumb idealist. I'm a shameful cad for running out on you — okay — you're in a position of some buying and selling. Weigh the good qualities against the bad. Buy that which will give you the most of what you desire. Again, getting down to the brutal facts which are, to say the least, disgusting –

I offer nothing but a pig-headed dreamer — when the conflict is ended there will be even less because I'll no longer be a dreamer!—

Here's the story and let's settle it once and for all time — and by heaven's let's not continue discussing this matter – I want to marry you – to spend the rest of my life with your telling me to stop biting my fingernails — when? — tomorrow, if it were possible—the day after the "duration plus six months" definitely! — Now we place the dilemma in your lap — you choose the most suitable time!—

The more I write the more confusing I get—even to myself! —

Today we went through a very dull R.S.O.P. — we've done this so often it isn't funny — R.S.O.P. – always called "arsop" Reconnaissance, Selection, Occupation of Position — Dull to say the least —

I phoned mom tonight – I'll try to get you later this week – say, when is Mother's Day. —

Next time I mention what we did during the day tell me to keep my mouth shut — that's restricted information—"for those people concerned only."

Darling, the radio blares forth that "Romanian Rhapsody" Enescu – recall the Russian Kretchma, the violinist, the soul stirring crying, spirit rising, swift music. — Memories hide thyself!!! How unfair to come after me thus!!! I love you.

> Your —
> and I do mean your
> Sid

In the spring the battalion moved to Camp Swift, near Bastrop, forty miles south of Austin, Texas. After a description of his location, Sid had some questions of his own, in response to some of mine.

April 28
Darling—
"Wake Island!" That's what they call this place. "Wake Island!!—An isolated island, miles from civilization, miles from the heart of the camp.— A wilderness clearing for special troops. No, I'm not joking. It is generally agreed that in order to go to the post movies one should carry a sack lunch and travel on a compass azimuth. ...This Sunday, duty permitting I'm going to Austin—

How to get there? Where to go? What to do?—Well—I'll let Austin decide it for me.—Strange—

I wonder, may I too ask questions? May I too speculate?—Can I ask for estimation of our position?—Will you love me as much as previously? Will _you_ romp once more in the snow? Will you be willing, as before, to fight side by side with me for _our_ future? Or am I being a silly boy once more—Probably— Let's not get too far apart, let's not lose each other—our love, our comradeship lets hold on—hold –

To have you near once more—to whisper inane bubbles into your ear—to kiss you—to have your shoulder as a pillow once more—what else could a humble soldier ask for—God, I pray for a leave—I pray fervently!!

I want you—to be with you—

> I love you.
> Your
> Sid

And he did get a leave! It was not enough to be "engaged-to-be-engaged." With Sid expecting to be sent overseas very soon, he wanted a more official commitment.

May 3, 1943

Hyah — Ought to be home for extremely short leave beginning the 8th — I'll try to fly home — leave so very short it's cruel — 10 days — disgusting — about five days home. I repeat —

Will you marry me??? Yes??— no??—

—Your Sid

On May 11 Sid arrived home. Doubts and fears disappeared with the first ecstatic embrace. That evening there was a blackout, which we spent clutched in each other's arms in Sid's oversized arm chair. On May 14, Sid knelt in Central Park and put on my finger the engagement ring which we had chosen that day, with a knot of passers-by looking on as interested spectators. It was an unbelievably happy moment. That evening, Sid's fraternity brothers congratulated and toasted us. On the following night, at the Claremont Inn, a mansion overlooking the Hudson River converted into a restaurant, we had a very special dinner followed by dancing on the outdoor patio. On May 16 he returned to Camp Swift, Texas, where his training continued.

Company D
82nd Chemical Battalion. (Mtz.)
Camp Swift, Texas
May 21, 1943
Darling—

A strange, glorious tale it is! With all the dramatic episodes found in a thrilling love story magazine two individuals become engaged. A blackout, a row boat ride, an unsurpassable proposal all entered into the plot. Finally, though, he convinced her that money, brains, and good looks weren't everything in life and slipped the magic ring (solitaire, emerald cut, .91 carat!) onto the fourth finger from the right on her left hand. (It gets complicated!) — Ye Gods what floating free light emotions !! — I must have my shoes filled with lead to keep me from going completely up in the air — Yep — I'm happy too.

You'll excuse incoherent wanderings. I can't for the life of me get myself to concentrate, especially when I think of you. —Mushy??—hmmmm …

Your — always your
Sid

Sid had asked me to get him an identification bracelet and a ring, which I was delighted to do. But they weren't ready yet. He asked about

75

them in his letter of May 26 because, he wrote, "time is so short!!— This outfit is hotter than a frying pan on a stove!"

Life at Camp Swift, Texas, provided occasions for humor and for compassion.

June 3
Sweet!—
     …Yesterday we had a mock court-martial—I was the defendant— All wanted to know why I couldn't, during the 1 hr. or so blackout, talk you into getting married? — All insisted that there was too much talk and not enough action!!—It finally wound up by their deciding that they were a Section Eight Board, and that I was crazy as a loon and should be given a mental disability discharge!!!—Frankly it was a riot!!!—You— notorious?—Hell yes!! —
     I love you, my darling—"extensively" (you know what I mean— Huh??)
     We've received some new replacements recently—I feel so old when I look at these kids their taking into the army now.—When I first entered the battalion we had all those physical misfits and old men—All gone now.—I couldn't help getting a lump in my throat when I watched one kid—18 or 19 address a package to his mom—It was all his unessentials going home—
     They're so naïve—so unawares of the army world!—So interested in doing well—They still haven't developed that "damn everything!" attitude ——My company commander gave one of them his customary "talkings"—The poor kid had tears in his eyes as if a school teacher had put him on a dunce stool!!—Ah-yes—the er — — "tender age!"…

Say — you
I love you.
Your
Sid

Sid now had the ring I had ordered for him. When I said I hoped he would really want to wear it, he replied, "Are you kiddin'???—Of course!!"

June 9

Darling

At present I'm entirely at peace with the world. The sun is fading in the west. Someone's radio whispers a torch song in the distance. In the southern skies tall white billowing cumulus clouds pyramid themselves toward heaven. An officer passes. His pajamas droop in the fashion of a baby's diapers….

Me?—I'm just looking at your ring—admiring the ring—loving you—as always I do—

Its now 8:05—or 2005—The radio— "Let's Get Lost" —whatta ya say??—

Darlin'—I just finished a conversation with Capt. Greene. It ran something like this—

"So you're engaged!"

"Yep!"

"When ya getting married?"

"Oh—I guess after the war!"

"Did you ever hear of the War of Roses?—Lasted one hundred and 3 years—didn't it."

A disgruntled— "hmm—hmm."

My darling –If I don't get a chance to phone on Saturday night—know I love you—That I'm happy for you—and love you—and what the sam hill did we talk about "about a year ago." Yoiks! — —

Happy, happy birthday—success—alone now—success, later,—with me!!!—

I love you

Your

Sid

Sid was about to be sent overseas from San Francisco as a member of a 4.2 mortar unit attached to the infantry.

Morale was shaken by news reports of coal strikes in West Virginia, race riots in Detroit, and fights involving Mexican youths wearing the loose-fitting suits known as "zoot suits."

Co D 82nd Chemical Bn. (Mtz.)

A.P.O. 4573 — c/o Postmaster

San Francisco, California

June 24

Darling.

…Frankly, there is so little to say. Our daily schedule goes on. I still, as always, spend my spare moments thinking of you. Occasionally a thought or two on the stupid and rotten universe upon which we were placed. 'Stelle—am I wrong? Am I being disillusioned—What's all this in Detroit?—The coal mines? The Zoot Suiters? Strikes—Here we are at the verge of consummating our patriotic "duties" and that nonsense goes on to goad us in the back.

'Stelle I'm a rational human being. You and I quite understand each others sentiments. Ye Gods—Do I have to watch my men sweat, strain, curse—yes even, sometimes cry out in utter exhaustion as has happened—And yet attempt to keep a straight face when I read the morning papers…

What's going on in the above mentioned places is not a question of social problems—Its rank selfishness!!!!…

Keep me posted—Keep mail coming at all times—

Darling—just remember—no matter what happens.—Past, present, or future—I want you—

Your

Sid

After what he had said months before about the dangers of serving in a 4.2 mortar unit, and also about serving with the infantry—("They die like flies in the infantry")—hope for a happy outcome seemed very fragile. Sid's last letter from the States voiced his deepest hopes and resolutions.

June 25, 1943

For once I'm going to write slowly and carefully. This evening I must weigh my words and come forth with a clear statement. There must be nothing equivocal. Nothing which may be misconstrued or challenged. You and I, now, must forget all past, present, even future petty emotions. Now, you and I, as two individuals are faced with the problem of making definite statements – Here is my creed; my articles of faith!

1. No matter what the turmoil and confusion of body and soul I will remember our mission for a prolonged and happy life together. I will!
2. I will return to you!
3. If by some will of some one other than of this Earth I be injured I will bear it like a gentleman — I will! I shall leave this life if necessary the way I tried to live — with honor.

Please keep this "creed" for moments when a hearty laugh is required ….

One of the P.X. girls noticed your ring today— "That's a peculiar looking ornament."

"Oh—my fiancée gave it to me and also this"—whereupon I shoved my right hand under her nose with the bracelet. She gasped "How wonderful!"—Me—brilliant boy—gulped— "It took five years of patient work!"—A dirty look was my well-deserved reward....

'Stelle—be good—wait for me—love me—

Your

Sid

The troop ship left San Francisco on June 27. Sid took notes on the long journey, to share it with me as best he could, sending me finally 34 pages of his "journal." Excerpts follow.

Darling,

We've been at sea for several days now. After much procrastination and self-admonishment I've finally convinced myself that now is the time to begin writing. I've finally acquired my sea-legs and, what's more important, a relatively stable sea stomach.

Let's begin the saga with the present. The Pacific now plays havoc with all who invade her privacy. Huge frightening swells rise in the horizon and advance towards us like thundering herds of horses, galloping fiercely! They attain unbelievable proportions as they come closer....The swell breaks into an angry white-cap. The bow of the ship lists to the starboard. Her port side is raised violently into the air. Down, down goes the right until one can almost touch the foaming waters below...slowly and inevitably she rights herself once more—and so the battle continues. Man against sea....

Our worthy vessel, though, continues on her way. Despite the constant pitching, swaying, veering, backing she plods steadily onward. Ever her bow points towards the new country and our destiny!...

The most fascinating of all sea fowl is the albatross. Several of this species accompanied us out to sea. It fills one with tremulous admiration to watch them volplane along. They scarcely ever move their wings. Deriving their lift from the air currents near the waves they swoop literally inches from the waters surface and glide back and forth, turning by banking to the right or to the left, their wing tips just skimming the crest of the waves.

After we were out a day or so we were met by a school of porpoise which according to sea legend is an incident meaning good luck on the voyage....

We continuously frighten small groups of flying-fish.—These fish who don't fly!—Deriving a tremendous forward force from their powerful tail they thrust themselves up into the air and glide for what seems an endless period of time....

Another source of interest and diversion is the nocturnal visit to the deck.—I've continuously looked for stars but it seems as if the sky is always overcast. One very astonishing phenomenon is the flashes of light from the plankton on the surface of the water. Plankton as I get it are tiny living organisms which exist on the surface of the ocean. They give off a luminescent light when startled. 'Stelle its absolutely exciting to watch these tiny flashes of brilliant dazzling light....

I've just returned from a shower....You with your skid-proof baths, your handsome mats, your solid steady floors!!—Try, if you can to imagine taking a shower—as you stand in the tub, the floor suddenly rising beneath you, then suddenly lurching away towards the right down!—One returns from a shower with innumerable bumps and bruises—Occasioned perhaps by bending down to wash a knee—the ship rolling—and then smashes one headlong into the wall!...

You guess of course that the situation is being exaggerated but when I tell you all fear of submarines is forgotten when one braves the shower room, believe me!...

This is some days later. This is what I call one of my "other" afternoons, You see the routine of day calls for First—Remove outer garments— Second Remove underwear—Wash underwear immediately. Using three suits I manage to wash clothes every "other" day.

The heat has been growing steadily more intense, more oppressive. During the day we perspire— In the night we toss and turn and sweat....It does feel like a "warm-up" for a trip to hell!...

My days are gradually becoming more and more full!—Inspections, some study—some sleep—some drills (which always come when one is half-way undressed or in the climax of a good story.)...

Oh for something to break the annoying sameness of each day. Ocean trips or no ocean trips I crave a change. The discomfiture is all the more intensified by the heat which pounds one's body continuously. Sticky, sweaty heat which galls a man.

Last night for the first time we could see the stars. Remember our trip to the Hayden Planetarium. Recall the Southern Cross the lecturer stressed so much. Well—at last I've seen it....

Somehow, at present, I'm overcome with a fit of homesickness. I'd like to conceal it. I'd like not to wander into sob acts like some crone singing maudlin songs but well—that's the way I feel!...

How's the "warbling" Mrs. Spero getting on—Strange how a retrospection makes all those nights seem so "nice," so gay—How I feared your mother!!—Poor querulous idiot—I mistook genuine interest on her part to be animosity. Now, with the waves washing the sides and the ship's engine purring I realize how grateful I should be to your parents for putting up with this—well lets call him "soldier"—They also get the "swell people"…

I'm a bit curious about Oscar. That A11 .91 or was it .95 emerald-cut diamond—Has it the same luster—sparkle?—What's most important— Does it have the same meaning??

> I love you
> Your
> Sid

Arrived okay –in South Pacific

At sea—Somewhere in the Southwest Pacific
Darling—

I love you!—Quiet—no protests! no idiotic statements! When I say I love you its final—period! And we'll have no discussion about the matter! And we <u>will</u> be married as soon as I return——**Quiet!**—We'll have no interruptions!…

Back to the amphibious Diamond and his new adventure on the high seas. (I do mean high) The old boy walks about like an aged hypochondriac. What with taking my daily atabrine pill, a dose of bisimuth and paragoric for the stomach, the dread of sea sickness, the oppressive heat— "A soldier's life is not a happy one!"—It's a bit exaggerated. My intestinal disturbance is gone. I'm back to fighting trim.

These are "dangerous waters." You will scarce realize how little we fear our yellow friends, their submarines, their airplanes.

Strange thing—the master and crew of the vessel are superstitious. They've asked us not to whistle or sing. Whistling or singing brings bad luck. The astonishing thing about it all is that my father always used to stop me when I whistled in the house for the very same reason!!!!

'Stelle when I return I want, besides you, a tall, cold glass of sweet milk, then a tall vanilla malted!! (I've had no fresh milk since we left the states.)

By the time [of] my tour of duty in this theatre I ought to be quite a seaman.

We've six officers squeezed into one stateroom. At night when all windows are closed tight the smoke from pipe, cigars, cigarettes hangs heavy in the cabin. We've named it "The Opium Den." For one dollar you can get a pipeful of Tobacco and a bunk to sleep and dream…The Den is complete with password, ... and countersign. It has a blue atmosphere producing blackout light—

This afternoon some gang from a nearby cabin labeling themselves F.B.I.—invaded our "den of iniquity"—er—haunt of debauchery and confiscated several bars of smuggled Macey's chocolate bars!!

I'll quit now—duties to perform—

I love you—

> Your
> Sid

The ship arrived at the port of Noumea, New Caledonia on July 19. Sid was not yet allowed to name this island, but there was enough information to enable me to guess where he was.

July 26

Darling!—

I find that I may mention a great deal more about my surroundings and activities than previously, consequently, you'll have to sit through another barrage of "This's and That's"

I'm located on a large island in the southwest pacific. The language spoken on the island is French!!!—Don't think I haven't been brushing up on the little French I once knew!!—Well to get on with the data. There are blacks and some black soldiers. The natives go around barefooted—the black native soldiers wear leggings but no shoes.

This is coming almost verbatim from the "Things that can be mentioned" list.

At present we're building a base camp.—by the by—I've had a most fascinating experience in the field of ceramics—or mud-pies to you!—I'm supervising the construction of an incinerator for my company. One of the essential parts of the incinerator is the stack. I'm trying to pack mud about a mold, then allow it to bake in the sun. Using the bible as my guide, I've had straw mixed with the mud and have added a good deal of prayer to the work....

This island is almost entirely free of fever!!! No malaria, cholera, or any of the other hateful tropical diseases.—It's the truth so help me! The island abounds in deer, wild pigeon, fish, mountains, coconuts, guavas, oranges, lemons, bananas, cactus, long grass, eucalyptus. There are no land snakes to speak of....

An incident which occurred in town—I struck up a conversation with one of the girls taking care of a lemonade stand—It was all in French mind you, I was doing pretty well too.—She caught sight of your ring and immediately asked if I was married!—I told her I was engaged and promptly produced your picture. "Very pretty" she exclaimed! "How come all American boys are married or engaged to pretty girls?" All I could do was shrug my shoulders.—Then I had some ice cream—very watery but good!

Can't use the French—no foreign languages allowed in out-going mail....

I feel quite elated at this opportunity to use some French—poor as it may be. The difficulty there, of course, is the few opportunities one has for visiting—...

My striker or orderly knows you or should I say your picture by now. As soon as I pulled it out he remarked—"You want it here facing you when you write letters?" And that's where you are—a bit in the shadows but still present—

Darling—remember—always,

> I love you
> Your
> Sid

Late in July Sid wrote of being jumped "temporarily" to company executive officer. The parting from his platoon was painful and emotional on both sides. "There was a deathly silence when I left!!"

Training on the use of guns and mortars and the setting up of observation posts intensified

I was still not able to accept with equanimity Sid's having risked our future together before it was required of him. And I was unable to keep my fears to myself. One of my letters elicited an angry reply: "Perhaps I don't understand—I know I'm not the best guy you can get....If you change your mind in any way—remember—I want you to be the gentleman and let me know....I used to think the only safe and indisputable points in my existence were the respect of my parents and our mutual affection. I could be wrong." The next day he felt obliged to reconsider.

Co. D 82nd Chem.. Bn. Mtz.
A.P.O. 502 c/o Postmaster
San Francisco, Cal
Sept. 11, 1943
Darling-
   ...I feel like a heel!!...

After the usual cool deliberation all I can do is kick myself in the pants and say, "Who are you to talk. Yes, you're the one. Talk a girl into an engagement when you knew damn well you mayn't see her for months, perhaps years, afterwards. Whisper plans of a future when deep inside there's a trembling question. What do you know besides ways and means of killing? What sort of work could you do?

What about your education, pal? Will you be patient enough to plod through a few more years of school? Has your never-too-good mind been so thoroughly dulled and rusted by mud, rain, boredom, and repetition that it is never to function efficiently again? How can you be RE-habilitated upon return when you'd never established a definite place for yourself. Is there a slot somewhere for you to fill or will you, like many soldiers before, wander aimlessly—endlessly seeking your place in the world. A world at peace has no place for a soldier.

Ideals?— Dreams?—Those have all been shattered to a pulp a long time ago…. Yes, you're convinced it was a necessary war— Yes, you've weighed the social, political, economic reasons carefully and can realize the inevitability of it.—Yes, yes—yes!!—but damn it—what about yourself??"

Darling, I've gone over those things very carefully. I can't answer them to my own satisfaction. Perhaps that's the reason why I blew up?… I don't know. 'Stelle, please understand, now I've got a job to do, a responsibility — —come hell or high water I'm going to do it!!!…

'Stelle—of what use is it for me to cry out my loneliness. Words, rhetoric, all could never possibly describe the emotions which haunt me day and night. If mental telepathy existed you'd find your days and nights full of messages….Miss you?—Darling, do the stars still shine over New York? Is the moon as bright? Does the Harlem still flow?—…'Stelle, darn it all, I miss you so terribly and can't do anything about it!!!—

> I love you.
> Your
> Sid

Sept. 22

Its Tuesday morning. I've just grabbed the nearest sheet of paper and begun writing. Same place as before; same situation. Clerk, first sergeant, company commander, and switchboard operator fill in the bare spots of the stage. You can see the company doing calisthenics off in the distance. A faint Hup! hoop! Heep! Haw! is heard. A truck brings in a large container of water. The drama of the day is about to proceed.

Lets skip the "drama" and get down to the week-end which has passed. Adventure, excitement, hair-breadth escapes, climaxes, dare-devil rescues, anti-climaxes, all packed into two days of "Dick Merriwell" type experiences. It may sound a bit exaggerated but that's the way it happened.

Saturday afternoon tortured by ennui and questing something different three officers, myself and four sergeants loaded into a jeep and small truck for a hunting and fishing trip. We were packed in amongst bedding rolls, equipment, rifles, pistols, automatics, food. We returned Sunday night bedraggled officers, two completely naked and I, soaking wet!! The rest stranded with the trucks.!!

It started in a usual manner, a rough trip across the mountain; several streams forded, supper of steak, fried potatoes and coconuts we gathered. We made arrangements to use a life boat for fishing the next day. The boat was an old whale boat with a motor and superstructure added. Never will I forget that boat!

Saturday night we decided to gather some bait. It was the most ridiculous unorthodox fish "hunt" the imagination could conceive. Imagine me, waste high in the water, hat on, pipe in mouth, shirt and field jacket still on. Shoes and socks finished my "fishing outfit." Flashlight in left hand, automatic in right I stalked the fish near shore. As soon as I saw the white of a fish skimming through the water I'd sight the flashlight down the barrel of the automatic and fire. In this manner we picked up a good deal of bait.

Sunday, the great day, …we were under way. Fishing was excellent. Just throw a line in and wham you'd land a fish! Suddenly our troubles began. Troubles which have not yet ceased. It started with a slight drizzle. We had light rains before so we ignored it. Then, then it came. A hurricane!!—a small one I'll agree but from where we were it was like a major upheaval.

The wind howled. The waves grew to gigantic menacing mountains. The coconut trees swayed. We watched the waves crash against the reefs. Our boat pitched, tossed, rose, fell. The waves played havoc with our little boat. The men slipped, banged against the side. We all held on for dear life as the waves broke over us.

As usual in such uncomfortable situations we'd joke. The men whooped as if they were riding broncos. I remarked "It was just like a row in Central Park!" The motor failed!!!

Our hearts stopped as the engine ceased throbbing. …The distributor lines were wet. Hastily we dried them with gasoline and sighed comfortably as the engine resumed her put-put-put. She failed several times after that but we were able to keep her going.

About this time we were all getting a bit ill. I was the first to grow very ill....Every time I'd open my mouth I'd get a spray of salt water to add to my discomfort.

We finally reached shore, drenched, tired, sick, but safe.

Our troubles had only just begun. After warming up and eating at a nearby army unit we started home. We traversed a cruel torturous twisting and winding road around and over the mountain. It still amazes me how our vehicles stuck to the road. Several times we'd slip off the road but managed to fight our way back...We were finally stopped by a small stream which had swollen to a roaring, turbulent, angry, and swift river. It was impossible to cross. We turned back to try the only other route across the mountains.

To reach this road there was a long race across the beach. Cliffs on one side, rising sea on the other we ran the "gauntlet" to the other road.... Again we were stopped by a ford which had grown to a perilous swirling roaring river.

Someone had to return to camp to get food and help. Without waiting I asked if someone would go with me—No one would.—I waded, fully clothed into the stream, swam and fought my way across. The swift current carried me 50 yards downstream before I reached the other side....

I finally reached the main road. I was picked up by a passing marine in a jeep. At camp I gathered some equipment food and help and started back to the stream.

Back at the crossing we strung a line across the stream and tried getting the commanding officer across on a raft. In the center of the stream the current pulled the raft from under him. Fortunately he was able to pull himself across on the line we'd strung across. The other officers pulled themselves across on the line and we left the rest of the men to guard the trucks.

Yesterday we sent a crew back to look for the equipment lost when the raft upset. Most of it was recovered. Last night the stream subsided sufficiently to allow us to get the trucks back. Everyone's home—everyone's safe.

Me—I'm still the silly boy that loves you—very extensively. And ye Gods 'Stelle lets both snap out of it—your letters and my own are beginning to sound like the rumblings of an approaching storm. Let's get in out of the rain. Perhaps my letters sound a bit grouchy—forgive me,— please.—I-I-just am lonely for you. My thoughts are always interrupted by you—You're constantly before me. Every time I do or say something unpleasant unconsciously I remark "'<u>Stelle</u> wouldn't like me to act this way!"—If I grow angry it definitely is because I <u>want</u> to be with you and can't tolerate your heckling about what I could have done to stay. Instead of kicking myself in the butt for being a damn idiot I make a mess of the whole thing—Darling—seriously—I love you—irrevocably—

Yours—and yours alone
Sid

Christmas?—er—cigarette lighter? New toilet articles kit? <u>Picture of you???</u> Moccasins? (really anything—even nothing but that you still love me will do)

In late October, after a sea voyage to Guadalcanal, no longer the site of battle, training and preparation for Bougainville, in the Solomon Islands, resumed in earnest. Sid would be sent there in a few weeks. His concern for our relationship and my happiness were very much on his mind.

Oct. 21
Darling,

Its late. I should be asleep. I must write.

Today has been a very uneventful affair. Nothing has occured to disrupt the sameness of our existence here. Bored? Homesick? In love with you? I'll leave those questions for you to answer.

This afternoon I played around the motor pool. You know I still haven't got my government drivers license. True I've driven everything that's come my way from jeep to 21/2 ton truck. But never "legally." I know one fact. I'm only a backwoods driver and would never made a good city driver. Give me a wide open road with plenty of room and I'll be in heaven.

The trucks are the most amazing creations. One scarcely can conceive of the amount of energy required to manipulate one of those huge lumbering monsters. My greatest difficulty is getting used to the double-clutching necessary to shift gears. Problems, problems—will they never cease!

I've not received any mail from you today. No—I'm not complaining. You've been swell as far as the mail is concerned. I'm just curious about the storm we've been hatching amongst ourselves. — Sweet—lets make this thing simple. A guy and a gal in love. — period!! Okay?

Don't, don't ever worry about me and my feelings. Don't try to be noble and sympathetic. I'm a big boy now. Whatever's coming my way—let it come! From bullets to facts!!!—

Have fun—enjoy whatever you can. Have enough fun for both of us. Take it all in. One of us should have bright and pleasant surroundings. One of us should have the pleasures I've denied us. — Do it because I want you to; because I couldn't stand the thought of you home alone, growing into womanhood without all the pleasures rightfully yours. Know that I'll never condemn you for anything except wasting your life as a result of my stupidity....

I love you —
Sid

One can see from this letter that twenty dollars went pretty far in 1943!

Darling —

Enclosed you'll see a postal money order for $20. Wait—and listen—before you object. This is not a gift. It is not for Chanukah, Christmas, New Years or the Dance of the Seven Veils. I'm sending it to you for a definite soul satisfying reason. Hear me out beloved. (Never used that before—corny!)

It's a date—see? Take the twenty and have a roaring good time. Imagine that I'm with you and go to town. There are certain favors, if so they may be called, that I request. Please follow the following program.

1. Some Friday night soon get together with a friend, (preferably female—all other kinds are acceptable, but inferior).
2. At 6:30 sit down to a tremendous supper to include steak, fresh vegetables, luscious creamy strawberry shortcake.
3. Go to a theatre—any one will do. No, —no musicals allowed. Something light.
4. Oh—make sure you both have corsages (if the other is that kind)—at least you have one.
5. Downtown both order a tremendous dish of ice-cream. Make it last long. Play with the ice cream—smack your lips—say ah—ah—ah————ah!—
6. Drink a tall glass of ice water and treat it like champagne.
7. On the way home purchase a can of SPAM and a can of VIENNA SAUSAGES.
8. At home—you play Nocturne.
9. Then both of you rub your hands in fiendish glee. Laugh ghoulishly.—Open the cans of Spam and Vienna Sausages, empty them into the garbage can; curl imaginary moustaches; and with a tremendous howl of bloodthirsty madness—place

the cover on the can and rejoice in the killing of mankind's scourge! (This mankind!)

10. The rest of the money spend foolishly—If there's anything practical or intelligent about it—ignore it—you musn't do anything that isn't within my usual Friday nights routine— —(If it's a He I'll permit the ignoring of the lengthy good night!)

11. At 12:00 P.M. you might talk your mother into whistling!

Okay?—It's a date—Let me in on the sordid details. I was going to request that that you roll in the snow, but, well, you're a big girl now.—

Today we worked alongside some of the native boys…

One boy approached me.

"You sellum boy ring?"

I replied, "No can do."

"One boy like much ring."

"Ring belongum number one girl me. Number one girl belongum me. No sell one boy ring. Like much much number one girl me!"

Pidgin English is worse than French. Superlatives are expressed by duplication—hence "much much nice" or "pretty pretty"…

I could use some stationary. Please get the envelopes with stamps already on. Its close to impossible to pick up that stuff.—

Oh yes—while you're being so helpful—and you are!(my mother'll kill me for asking you to do all this)—A wristwatch strap will come in handy. Mine is broken. …

I love you much much number one girl.

Your

Sid

It hardly takes reading-between-the-lines to feel the despondency in the following letter.   A.P.O. was Sid's fraternity at City College.

Nov. 18

Darling—

Ye Gods and peppermint candy what a mail!! After weeks of going batty with worry and loneliness I get a deluge of long delayed letters. Manna from heaven! Most welcome, of course, were yours—yours of Oct. 14, 18, 25, 26, 30. At least I know you're still alive,—I've already read them three times and am already planning an evening of pleasure rereading them. —

In regards to "that" picture where you lie supinely, your right hand over your eye with that "come hither and I'll show you" look—-Comment?— Who's the crumb who took these.—I smell a male—I don't like his or her artistic leanings.—Me!—a prude??—There are no prudes thousands of miles from home!—where there are no women to be seen.—I just don't go for this pin-up gal stuff.

Damn it—somethings wrong or very right about me lately. I can't take anything seriously. Everything tickles me. I chuckle at each man who moans about his girl's leaving him. The best is the boy who'd already purchased the furniture and she married someone else. South Pacific blues!! Sorry case!...

Allow me to interject a most hilarious bit of humor. Len K. is stationed in Fort Monmouth, N.J. He writes, quote "New York is starting to get on my nerves again—even after 5 visits in 4 weeks. All I do on a weekend is run around and knock myself out—result—exhausted all week!!"...

I've discussed Len's remarks with the gang. Overwhelming opinion— "What booby hatch has he escaped from!"...

You've anticipated one of my questions. In an A.P.O. bulletin they mentioned Claire and Dave getting engaged—That was dated Oct. 5— Three weeks later I hear they were married—Never did believe in long engagements myself—People should always marry within 5 years after they get engaged—If they wait longer hardening of the arteries seriously hinders happy married life...Give them my "blessing" and damn it—I'm jealous— —Oh well—think of it—In the years to come when they've come to the stage where he goes to the movies and she to a mah-jong gathering you and I will still be holding hands and being desperately in love(???)...

Speaking of photographs don't let my silly cracks stop you from sending photographs—I like 'em—er—some of 'em.

Politics, military affairs, committees, the senate, congress, executive legislature—all a pile of words—All I'm interested in is getting this over with—now! Send us the guns, the men, and plenty of ammunition.—We'll tend to the other punks when we return.—Me?—It's all so ridiculous—so funny—so ludicrous!!

I love you, darling!

Your

Sid

Maintaining our relationship despite the stress of time and distance apart was difficult, but not impossible, given Sid's humor, understanding, and love. Having graduated from Hunter College in June, soon after our engagement, I was now working at Bell Laboratories on equipment for the war.

Nov. 25

Darling—

This is that old rake Diamond, your fiancé (one "e") bowing humbly and pleading once more. I've begun this on onion skin paper which indicates a definite trend towards a long letter with a grand amount of begging!…

Let's reconstruct a scene—an actual one. It's a camp just out of the jungle. Pup tents neatly lined up, kitchen cheerily welcoming all with odors of hot chow. A weary, bedraggled, hollow-eyed column makes its way into camp.

"Mail Call!"—No longer is there fatigue. No longer do they slouch. News has come.

The lieutenant quietly sits aside with his all too precious letters. Yes one is from his favorite girl. Yes of course there is a smile, a hope, an anticipation of a pleasant interlude with his love. Men glance knowingly in his direction. They all know, by now what that peculiar shaped ring on his left hand signifies. He reads!

What—his girl is unhappy! Unhappy because of his own actions! He has caused a worry to plague his already so mistreated wife-to-be. He no longer can think. The jungle and the tropics have sapped his strength of mind and body. How—How can he make her understand? How can he keep her from that burning revolt which comes to everyone in love? — He doesn't know. His frank, ingenuous description of his existence, down to the very letters he receives, cause unhappiness.

Darling—darling—please—please—try to understand. Try to comprehend that your happiness means more to me, now, than life itself. Try to see that anything you wish, desire, will be my ambition. Know that when the flying foxes awaken me by their squeaking it is you that keeps me from falling asleep. You—no one else. Ida, Penny, Mary—Cripes— kid—I wouldn't write of them if I were "deceiving" you! If you promise not to write a scathing letter making me feel like twice the idiot I am why there'll be no more communication between them and me.

I know—you'll immediately put yourself on the indignant defensive and become uncomfortably magnanimous. "Sid," you'll say, "Don't let me interfere. Go ahead—have fun, —enjoy life—blah—blah—blah"—Damn it, 'Stelle its our lives! I'm a fifty percenter in this deal! If something I do or say or hint or remark hurts or displeases I want to stop it!!!—Can you comprehend!!! —

Just like a ridiculous officer—making up for his mistakes by scolding others. Just remember if you're unhappy, I'm unhappy.

'Stelle, when the body and mind rebel in the inferno of this island— When the will is sorely tested as you slosh through the dense jungle; when ants cover your body and bite and scare you half to death. When your calves are covered with "jungle itch" (called sometimes "Jungle Krut" or Jungle rot); when your sleep is fevered and restless; when tremendous lizards pop up and cause fear to strike your heart— — then, then you know what holds you together. What makes you want to keep going. What makes you desire to fight everything so that you can survive and return. You, darling—you and you alone!

Quiet!!—Don't you go making simple statements that you are afraid of the responsibility!!

Four days and nights devoted to training in the jungle. Then up at 4:30 next A.M. to supervise work on the docks and unload ships. — Work all day in the maddening sun—Eat a tasteless supper—Read about a strike for higher wages and watch your men drag their bodies in after an exhausting eight hours of hard physical labor. Then go to an officers school for two hours. Prepare something for the next weeks training.—Worry about details of your men's comfort and health.

Darling, those things don't phase me if I knew all was well with you. That you and I were as ever. That you were still sure of my love—Nothing could make me quit!! Sweetheart—know one thing for a certainty — No body,—no thing, no past, present, or future is of any value to me if it doesn't include you!!

Be good—kid—take care of yourself—and please darling—don't ever doubt my affection for you.

Lost two buttons from my shirt while out in the jungle.—I've ferreted out your sewing kit...

By the way—as a sidelight.—I know now how invaluable you are.

After we returned from our session in the jungle I was greeted by your package. A delicious package of "Cut to Fit the Mouth" salt water taffy. 'Stelle it's the first soft candy I've had in a month. No one at home could appreciate the ecstasy of allowing the chocolate and filling to slowly melt in your mouth. Why, I ask you, should I tell you what I want? I would have requested [something] inconsequential like a lighter etc. But, it is you who knows what I really want. I'd never have thought of candy. Yet you've sent me a gift which brought untold pleasure. If I could only have you munching beside me, complaining about the untold calories, life would be complete!

Oh yes, I haven't explained the lack of mail—From the above information I think you understand why I couldn't write. Its 9:00 P.M. now. Bugle just blew taps.—Tomorrow I get up at 04:15 to go to the docks—Oh for a union!!

Here's something I would like you to send. It will prove of inestimable value to me. See if you can purchase a lantern of some sort which will operate on gasoline or kerosene. You know the kind that makes a farm look like a farm. It shouldn't be too large. I want it primarily for use at the base camp when I can read and write at leisure. The candles are killing my eyes. I can always get gasoline to fill it—Its very practical—very much needed—will be very much appreciated! Make sure its packed securely. Preferably in wooden box. Okay?

'Stelle—all joking and slush aside — you're a swell pal!

You are a constant source of amusement to my fellow officers. Firstly they can't understand how a punk like me rates a "dish" like you. I tell 'em you're after my money! (I don't know how I rate you myself!) –We usually spend long hours talking about the people back home. They know all my little problems. Whenever we talk of home they look at me and ask – "I wonder who's kissing her now?" Sunday afternoons, when its Saturday night back home they insist you're at the "Copa Cabana" or at central park with the engineer from the B.M.T. (their interpretation of B.T.L.) or out with "Young Doctor Kildare."

Me—Jealous?—Hell yes!! But that's beside the point.

Long, long letter—

I'm not displeased with you. I register my objection to the U.S.O. affair but—well—I asked for it! — —

I love you—You are my bestest gal what am!!

Your

Sid

P.S.— Look, included in the package I sent home—the one with the winter clothes—was an ashtray—It was made for me by one of my men. I want you to have it—The Knick-Knack or nick-nack kid he was known as.—

PS.PS.—Damn it—How I miss you!!

This island was definitely not Paradise!

Dec. 15

Darling,

Sweet—darling—you leave me so pleasantly good inside. I don't want ice cream. The devil with the rain. Give me a letter from my sweetheart!

Received your letters of Nov. 29 and Dec. 3. My poor misguided 'Stelle. There are no women here!!—Your "pals" labor under Hollywood delusions. The natives of this island took to the hills when the fighting took place. There are a slew of atrocity stories floating around about what the Japs did to all the women here. I walk around with a handful of salt to take with each new tale I hear.

'Tis true that some miles away, over a torturous road one can visit a small native village of twelve families. One visit is enough. The filth, vermin, deformed people, makes one say "Never again."

The natives we work with occasionally (males) –are intelligent… happy and, damn it, I like their independent attitude!!

The only attractive women, white or black, I've seen were in New Caledonia. So I'm engaged, so I don't mess around, so I'm a good boy, so tease and tell me I should've and I'll scream!…

Look, kid—I'm happy—in my own simple way. I want you to be happy—in your own way (complicated to beat all hell!)—You make living sound like an intricate difficult process.—You like something—take it!—Dislike something—cast it aside. Can't get something?—Oh well!!—See? Easy when you know how.

My love—my love—damn it all I love you so much.

Tomorrow we go into the jungle for a few more days of this man versus nature nonsense. Understand if there's no mail, huh?

Ah, yes The C.W.S. seems to have made the headlines. They tell me "Time" of November something had a write up of the 4.2 inch mortar. Also Saturday Evening Post of Nov. 20, a "fascinating" article entitled "Watch Our Smoke" …

Say, I wish you'd look around for articles about chemical troops in action. Send clippings to me.

Strange as it may seem you're a tonic. No bun—not the kind you use to slick your hair—more the kind that brings intoxicating pleasure! I sat down determined to write a short simple "Don't have energy or ambition—Love—Your Sid" Which was close to the truth. Once I started and began to feel close to you, when the tickling [from] your childish fears took hold, when I felt as if you were here—close by—listening—more probably not listening—but here—everything took on a new aspect. Darling, sweet—please, please get off my toes!!—No my pet – No you may not put your feet on my soap box!! Tsk – have some candy! Its good. The ants like it!

94

An army cot is not as luxurious as your couch but its comfortable. Its got a most annoying depression right at the small of my back. I shall soon walk like this picture ⨪ I do love you darling. Thanks for the visit.

I love you—you—I love you, I love you—I love you—

>Your
>
>Sid

Sadness and regret, not usual with Sid, seem to have taken hold, at least for a time.

Dec. 21

Darling—

Well—at last—nothing to say—I got up this morning—washed—ate—pancakes and prunes and coffee—returned to shave—remarked how ugly I was—wondered at this endless routine of shaving.

Reported to company—censored mail—Had long session with instrument men trying to convince them that you add an azimuth to get another one—or some such inane thing!—Talked to Plans and training officer about nonsense—Thought about you—

Placed some replacements into squads—gave them welcoming address—Strange how I've changed—used to be interested in making impression—Don't give a damn just as long as I get the job done.—Ever it was so with second Looeys.

Smoked a pipe—thought of the day I received it—Remember?—Fort Dix—poison ivy…So long ago—so very long ago.

God the sadist created his people to entertain him in this great theatre—Earth—…He's never called to task—yet every death, every hurt, every wound is an "Act of God!"—

Mail soon—Live from meal to mail call to meal—nothing else.—

I've found my soul—mom used to say a "sole" had to be stepped on before it can be of any use— —I'll wait—never found any use for it——never been trod upon—I find.—

How stupid I've been—What a child— —

Should have married you—should've—Too bad—strange—strange—"Strange Interlude"—Not so here—My name's not Gordon—or was that his name?— — I do forget easily—.

>I love you
>
>Your
>
>Sid

Sid begins by reprimanding me for not spending as he specified the $20 he sent. Considering the huge social, economic, and political problems which will need to be resolved, his morale is shaken, but not destroyed.

Dec. 30

Darling

Hello my fine feathered cur! Such "wanton" thrift is inexcusable.—That money order was for you—It was my small Christmas gift—I shall retire to my cubby-hole and drown my tears in tomatoe juice!!—bad girl!!—

Received your <u>long</u> letter of Dec. 13—only 17 days—we're improving!—Don't think that <u>that</u> typing goes unnoticed. The meaning is clear, the fine even letters, the margins well kept, no x's, no misspellings—Thanks—Thanks—

My dear young lady the question of when you and I will get married is beyond the arguing stage. There is no fight. The battle is over.—I've got you surrounded—outflanked—outmaneuvered—Besides I've got a big club to use in case of unforeseen resistance!!—My darling—much as I dislike being dogmatic with one so fair as thou—We will get married immediately upon my return—You needn't indulge in useless counterattack. The "jig's" up. See you before the judge—or rabbi—or High Llama—the day "after" for purposes of letting you place the ball and chain around my neck (your arms too!!)...

Your letters I get in bunches—weeks late. Seldes "In Fact" arrives promptly one per week.—I read, not to carefully, think two seconds—laugh—He tells nothing new or unsuspected.—Anyone with half a wit can understand what's going on. All these facts my gallant crusader are interesting—What are you doing about it??

Excuse me—but somehow this whole mess has become so overwhelmingly ridiculous. The stupid complexities of race, position, economics, labor, capital, religion, politics, resolve into one grand "Hellzapoppin" riot.—The human race isn't fine, good—its funny!!—humorous!! –Like a clown it goes through outlandish motions while its heart bleeds!!

There is no glory in mud, sweat, heat—There are no crusades—You've trained for years to become an actress—I play the lead in the greatest farce ever produced—the "Comedy of the Lord's Children!"— or—"What the hell!"...

'Stelle if anything happens to me know one thing—I've led a full pleasant life—I missed out on but one thing—marriage (that will be remedied the day I return)—I have no regrets…

Our Christmas was okay. A tree was manufactured by drilling holes in a tent pole and forcing palm stems into them—We had turkey with all the trimmings—The red cross gave us little Christmas packages—so much for that—

Forgive the unpleasantness of this ragged letter—I'm getting emotional—full of creeds and stuff again—

Dear, dear 'Stelle—I love you—

Your
Sid

Thanks for stamped envelope—only had one more air mail envelope left—I told you— we're on the same beam!! Come to think of it—Its astonishing!!—I really only have <u>one</u> left!!!

PART 3: 1944

The ebullience of Sid's early letters was now tempered by a deeper appreciation of what lay ahead. Strong in body and resolve, he was ready to lead men in battle. During an evening's respite from training, battalion officers gathered for a discussion of past experiences, and, most important, what kind of reception they could look forward to when they returned from the war.

South Pacific
Jan 2, 1944
Darling –

This morning I went into the jungle to inspect the impact area of yesterdays firing. My guns were on line but over by 50 yards.— I think its good. Particularly since it was impossible to see more than ten feet ahead and I ranged in by ear.—Me – the guy that couldn't tell a C from a C sharp trying to determine how far away a shell burst. – A new tune !!!

This afternoon Cotton, Hindman, and myself took two cases of empty beer bottles—our carbines and played Coney Island. We put the beer bottles up in trees, on the ground, on bushes. Then we just pot- shotted at the beer bottles.—It's like I said—this war business is an overgrown carnival— shooting gallery and all – Sunday was topped off by a "social" gathering of the remaining battalion officers. Everything from whores of Juarez to post war activities was discussed. Lt. Gutman raised this question—"What will the people back home say to us when we return? Will they call us suckers? They did those who fought in 1918!"—A strange hush fell over the officers, as if that was the question that all had thought about – all had worried about—We all realized how little people at home can conceive of the suffering, hardships, loneliness, violence of war. — We talked of the new generation—the teenagers that would look at their war tired brothers and fathers and speak of us as we once spoke of the men of the last war.— It wasn't pleasant—We knew then why so few veterans speak of their experiences.—no, not because they weren't exciting, new, dangerous — but because the squirts, the snot-noses, the know-it-alls had driven their souls to the background.

"What will we do if they call us suckers?" —

What will I do??—I often wonder—my equilibrium is a bit changed— Well—We'll see.

The young fathers wondered whether their kids would slam the door and run to mother shouting "There's a strange man outside!"—Captain Smith remarked, "You single men will have the biggest worry – how'll you get wives?—all your gals will be taken and the new ones won't go for your old fashioned stuff." I said,

"It may be old fashioned but that stuff will go any time, any place, ——
There's nothing new in that field."

We had egg-noggs – peanuts, cake, toast, cheese – Somebody's Christmas
packages just opened—I like these gatherings, particularly because they don't
play charades!!—Ugh!! —

Of course you and the Copacabana came up—damn 'em!—

Enough said—I love you—endlessly.

Your, Sid

*On January 3, Sid reported that he had been promoted to First
Lieutenant.*

Jan. 3

Darling,

I don't want to get "hoity Toity" or high falootin' but you're little bundle of
stupidity is now a first—er First Lieutenant!!—Yep, I'm off the gold standard
and now go in for silver bars. My orders came through today!...

My love—somehow my affection for you has changed—seriously—It
feels so much more satisfying, more mature—Its ripened. There is no longer
the uncertainty, the petty thoughts, the jealousies—the petty revolts of mind—I
think I understand— you, myself,—us. And I like it!!! Its warm, comfortable,
like walking into home after a day in the snow. Its like the thrill of clean clothes
after a march in the jungle.—At first I was shy about speaking of you. Now
my friends, officers—and I just start conversations with, "How's 'Stelle?" —
We're okay—With a minimum amount of interference and half a break we'll
be happy....

I love you.
Your
Sid

*On January 15, 1944, Sid's company, Company D, landed at Empress
Augusta Bay on Bougainville, and three days later Sid described what it
was like to be "greeted" by Japanese bombers.*

South Pacific

Jan. 18, 1944

Darling,

New A.P.O. – 706

I've received my "baptism of fire"; and a loud and merry one it was!!
– An air raid (we have them frequently) was the occasion. Old "Washing

Machine Charlie"— as the Jap bombers are called—came over to give us a "cheerful" greeting!—

It was night. We were wet. Hadn't been dry in two days. We were weary. Two nights of little or no sleep. The men were asleep in their hammocks. I dreamed on a wet cot—I tried to sleep but the dampness of my wet clothes chilled.

Then the alert!!! Lunged out of bed—no shoes—grabbed my helmet and literally dived into my hastily constructed fox hole. The Captain came in after me. Then high above could be heard the metallic drone of the planes. Strange – I wasn't too frightened—not then!—

Suddenly the Wagnerian Symphony of destruction began. All about the instruments of death blared into a tremendous crescendo. The tympanic section drummed forth the rhythm of terror. The sky lit up with all the poetry of bursting ack ack. World's Fair fireworks couldn't duplicate the uniqueness of a heaven studded with crashing red flashes. The tracers sketched the curves of Varga upon the Earth's ceiling.

In the intermission, Tojo played his quiet sad solo of the metallic drone.

I was so enthralled and awed by this pageant of Mars that I was caught dreaming when it came.—— A close strike—I could hear the bomb coming. I dived low. The Captain buried his head deeper in the hole.—wush- wush-wush **wush wush wush wush** WUSH WUSH WUSH——— BR-AMM!!! Then again—the growing wush and Bram! And again!—

I'll not say I was particularly cool.—Yes, I knew fear—The worst type of fear. Right then I "got religion"—so help me I prayed. —

As the raid progressed I stopped shivering. I grew calmer. I breathed more normally—Lt. Cotton & Hindman in a neighboring fox-hole started a cross conversation. Ted: "I wonder if that guy knows he could hit us." I said (classic remark) – "Probably not but I do!" ——— After that first scare why it all become commonplace, like seeing a horror picture the second time. I didn't care about the bombs. I wanted him to go home so I could leave my hole and "empty my kidneys." ——— My thoughts turned to things like the Lords Prayer and the weird jungle noises.

Then I breathed a deep sigh and cursed Tojo, Hitler, the plane, the dampness, the rain,— I cursed vehemently —

The all clear sounded and back to bed for a restless few winks. As you've no doubt surmised we're now in a combat area—There's little to fear. Yes there are Japanese soldiers around. —

Besides these air raids the "boom" of artillery in the distance keeps a man uncomfortable.

What I'm most interested in is mail from you. I haven't had a letter in two weeks—It will undoubtedly take time for the mail to catch up with me. —

In regard to air raids I wish I could be located at the probable targets of the Japs. So help me they couldn't hit the side of a barn at ten inches—Just drop eggs helter skelter, doing little or no damage except robbing us of sleep.

Yes—of course I love you—and am still determined to come home in one chunk and marry you —

Your

Sid

Jan. 21

Darling,

The situation continues as usual. The rain continues its incessant pounding on the tent top. Everything is wet, damp, moldy. All my clothes have that musty odor of rags left in a damp cellar to long. My person feels like the old water-logged plank that remains ever swished and swashed by the ebb and flow of the sea.

Old "Washboard Charlie" still comes around to keep us scurrying for our holes. Strange how accustomed I've become to "his" annoyances. 'Stelle, I marvel at his ability to miss our lines by so great a margin. The emperor seems to have fortunes to waste on indiscriminately tossing bombs over the empty jungle.

A few raids back I found myself dead asleep in a new location. I wasn't quite oriented with the general layout of the area. We'd had little sleep that night. The alarm sounded! Dreamy, half asleep, I jumped out of my cot.—I got out on the wrong side—catastrophic!! First there was the hurried groping for helmet.—No place was it to be found. Disgusted I felt my way to where I knew the hole must be—that is if I'd gotten out on the right side! Fortunately my hole mate shouted for me and I was able to slip into the fox-hole. See—getting up on the wrong side can prove unpleasant!!

Here's a beauty of an experience. The alarm sounded a bit late.—I jumped out—completely nude, grabbed my tin hat and flopped into the hole. Some "friendly" ants affectionately crawled upon my chilled body...

There is nothing else of consequence to be discussed.—Ah yes—your picture is out now. I feel more comfortable, more at home when I wander into the tent and there's your mien to remind me that there still are pleasant things, beautiful things somewhere in this world...

I love you—miss you overwhelmingly

> Your
> Sid—
> always.

The dates on the next two letters were not entirely clear.

Jan. 22

Darling.

Sweet—I do love you overwhelmingly. The days are long; the nights short. Sleep is a luxury. Good food a thing of the past. The war apparently progresses along its same slow lines. There is little if anything new to report. From the frequency of my letters you can surmise how little involved I am in any work. Gradually, we settle down to calmly fight a war. War is so much waiting, waiting, waiting!! Air raids now are commonplace dull affairs. Nobody gets hurt. Everybody curses the loss of sleep. Tojo wastes ammunition on nothing.

I am safe—I am careful—I am doing my job.

Occasionally there is that gnawing loneliness that drives a man to distraction.

I love you— "gigantically."—Be happy Sweet—

> Your very own
> Sid

Jan. 22

Darling

I'm going to get this off as hastily as possible—want to get some much needed slumber—Imagine my extreme elation when I returned recently and received three letters from you. The 27th and 30th—and the funny strips. First I'll answer your letters.

Envy, envy, envy—so Christmas gave you tremendous meals—enjoy 'em kid—

The hell with diet—you eat for both of us. Speaking of chow we received a new type of canned meat—I call it "Spam with personality."

The "In Fact" subscription. Of course I read 'em—of course I appreciated it—of course I know the NAM—etc. etc. etc. We see eye to eye on all these points only I don't enjoy pointless criticisms that offer no remedies...

105

'Stelle—my politics, if so they may be called are simple—I believe in man as an individual—a being entitled to certain privileges that he himself constructs for his own benefit—The unscrupulous, the cheats, the undesirables should be removed by the others—That the gov't as we now have it provides the people with that means—That they, the people, you at home, must keep your minds clear and active.—...

30th—Delightfully long and pleasant affair—accept many many kisses and embraces—you're okay! As they say in the army— "on the ball kid!"

You tell that gentleman Mr. Salomon that first—I object to his being so attentive to my sweetheart; second I object to the way he parts his hair (if he has any)....

Pictures—way off schedule—whatever you send will be cherished—the small one will go forward with me in my breast pocket. The large one will make my base tent seem all the more like home....

Medal of honor to you for the "conspicuous gallantry above and beyond the call of duty" in getting that Coleman lantern into the mails...

Your description of the basketball games was excellent. There you count number of balls through an iron ring. Here we score in lives. "Our team is red hot!!"

How about quitting and getting that M.A.—you know you want to!—Don't waste your time at that dismal place that so irks you....

I must close now—Darling—darling—Even "up there" I dream of you—hope for you—want you—when I should be observing I'm dreamin'—

Don't get excited—the apparent references to front line action are mere exaggerations of—a day's simple work—no—no danger—

Sweet—I love you—okay—so you go to U.S.O.'s—shrug shrug!!

> I love you,
>
> Your
>
> Sid

Feb. 1

Darling,

The lack of mail has been caused by-er-shall we say duty!—I've been in combat, front line stuff, participated in several pushes—still am—Only damages—dirty face, insect bites, weariness.

You talk of compatibility, of U.S.O.'s, of gifts, of things like politics, ideals.—I get caught under machine gun fire—snipers played hell all around—They'd zip, zip, zip above us. I held a lieutenant who insisted that he charge the gun. I gave him your "bear hug"—and kept whispering "take it easy boy, take it easy, take it easy."

I've seen "war" minus hollywood's beauty. Its not very pretty. The incidents of individual sacrifices, pains, hardships, heroisms, are so numerous but so difficult to talk about. I know now why so few "old timers" want to talk about their experiences. Civilians and U.S.O. soldiers can't possibly conceive of what actual combat is like.—

Enough said!...

'Stelle, I'm in a helluva mood but I've had a helluva time and don't particularly give a damn!—

I might add that your letters come regularly and are extremely welcome—

Believe me darling—I love you—

Your
Sid

Feb. 4

Darling,

I'm used to it by now. My nerves have settled down to their usual steady jangle. I can think a bit more clearly.

I vaguely recall that in the heat of the aftermath of an attack I wrote some inane, ridiculous, unkind nonsense. All I can say is it was unintentional, purely a result of some harrowing sights etc.

Please, please darling don't write anymore of people going to schools, of delaying their induction, of continuing their careers....

The promotion was received by dint of nothing but being a second lieutenant so long that the authorities got disgusted and booted me into a silver bar.

Sweet—there is little sleep on the line. Artillery fire etc. going all the time. Then there is the incessant fear of a Jap infiltrating into your position. I spend the silent hours of the night thinking, first of my men, of their security—then home and you. I do love you so much sweetheart. I do miss and want you. Just as I get to feel cozy, perhaps dreaming of you or I, a rat would go scurrying through the cane—I'd awaken fully—all senses alert—then back to sleep and you.

I feel so humble and reverent towards you.—To be with you and laugh once more—To sit with you and talk—To listen to you play the piano—To dance, drink cold drinks—read in comfort—to hold you in my arms—all these I want!!!—Play "Nocturne" just for old times sake!

I'm happy that you're going out and enjoying yourself. You're a swell egg!

Ah yes—you write of so and so getting hitched etc. etc.—Lt. Rubin (gossip) received a very neat little note from his heart burn wishing him luck and that she'd become engaged to someone else and that she hoped they would remain friends. Needless to say we all scoffed and gave him no sympathy! Ah yes—ah yes—ah yes—

"It can't happen here"—I hope, I hope, I hope.

Its pretty dull now. Nothing of any consequence has occured (occured? occurred?)

Yep—I love you—excitedly—

> Your
> Sid

Feb. 7

Dear darling 'Stelle,

Last night was torture. I kept dreaming and thinking of you. The past days have accustomed me to the unfounded fears of the war-neophyte.— Now I sleep comfortably and soundly —only—you— you—you keep haunting my thoughts. I fight sleep so that I may cogitate upon us.—

You are omnipresent. I feel the warmth of you—long to hold you close— want to hold hands at a theatre—I see your every feature there before me.— Remember this and that—The ridiculous quarrels—The ecstatic friendship and love—... Sweet—I do—do love you.

My abode—a hole capable of squeezing in 3 people—This is our command post at the mortar position—Sandbags stacked back, forward, side, and above—telephones hanging from loop—a table improvised from ammunition cases—some maps and a sheet of fire data.—I share this at night with Lt. Foster and a telephone operator—Kallor.

Kallor's a funny guy.—New York—Jewish—dress cutter—belongs to my father's union—Bachelor in early thirties—Knows all the angles and rackets of the dress line—... Also nearby is another interesting character.— Estes—The barber (not of Seville) ...He's a full blooded Cherokee Indian— Wants only to go home and finish high school. Seems that they go to school, that is secondary school, four weeks out of the year—the rest is occupied in work. He tells me that during the last war his tribe declared war on the Germans and have never come to peace terms.—...

Peculiar thing—you recall that incident of the machine gun rat-tatting over my head—I'll be damned if I didn't think how nice it would be if I were like you—no end!!—no end!!—Mine protrudes too too conspicuously!!—

Sweetheart—I love you extensively——

> Your
> Sid

Feb. 16

Sweet,

The rain plays pattering melodies on the tent top. The flame of the candle wanders like a woman in a bargain basement, hopping from side to side, not knowing which way to turn first. The turbulence is gone. All is still. All is well. The instrument sergeant doodles with some aerial photos I purloined this afternoon. The sergeant on one of my guns writes a V mail. I sit and slaughter whatever respect you've ever had for my prowess on the field of battle (contre typewriters).

One prepares for this great offensive by first making a few feints at the "roller-upper-knob." It clicks wonderfully. Encouraged, you make a few lightning thrusts at the "distance-from-the-edge-keeper-straighter." Some people call it by the ridiculous "margin stops"....

There are no apparent difficulties ahead so you set out a few fingers on patrol. To sort of feel out the keys and discover any information available. ...

So we make a strategic withdrawal along the poiiiuuytrewq trail and run smack into an ambush....The "Lock" and Ye Gods another "SHIFT." We are lost....We are surrounded....Shifts to the right of us. Shifts to the left of us volley and thunder....The question mark comes forward to help. A period here, a parentheses there, supported by a dollar sign. The keys fix bayonets. They jump from their holes. With a shout of "Banzai" and "MOIDA DA BUMS" they dash towards us. Armed with two very uncooperative arms, hampered by a lack of organization in the fingers...Give me a few more months in the wonderful south seas and I'll be completely batty.

You realize of course that this is getting me way past my bed time. You realize of course that you don't deserve this. YOU—You who go around getting New Yorker subscriptions behind my back. You who send trinkets. YOU Darn it I love you—I could hold you in my arms and literally smother you with kisses——and you say we'll wait to get married. My dear little one—my one and only one—I hate to have to commit mayhem or give you none to gentle taps on the skull with a crowbar, but "c'est la guerre" –and since there is little difference between the strategy of love and war we shall overcome all resistance by bold and brilliant strokes and our enemy's ability to fight back shall be demolished.

"Have you seen the light? Are you prepared?"

> I do love you,
> Your
> Sid

Sid was in battle off-and-on from January through April, and received two commendations. I was concerned that my letters, recounting only ordinary experiences of everyday life, might be found wanting. He explained his depression and the importance of my letters.

Feb. 25

My darling,

I've just torn up my fifth letter to the wife of one of my men. She wrote the company commander asking for details of the day when….Since it happened not fifty yards from me and he was acting with me I sort of felt a few lines from me might help—brave, courageous, gallant soldier. I've never realized the ridiculous emptiness of words until now. 'Stelle, I can't write it. What can my stupid inanities do for her? Yes, it might ease her mind, but there's nothing to replace him!— 'Stelle I feel like crying. All the sensation is there but no tears.——

Now—too—do I know how savagely unfair I was to ask you to become engaged. 'Stelle—I have your letter of the 15th—It would undoubtedly be best if I start from the beginning.

You say you recognize contempt and unconcern for the life of a civilian,—Somehow you believe that I'm bored with your letters—Sweet, nothing could be further from the truth. 'Stelle I just gave up momentarily— Nothing at all mattered—I was interested in nothing. As I've said such will never occur again.—In my own gruff way I was trying to share my anger and disgust but the words can never be spoken that will describe a soldier's thoughts during his first few hours of action.

Your letters are the luxury of this hell.— they are the cool refreshing breeze on a mountain top that blows away the cursed hot sweaty wild thoughts.—These letters are the links between me and the past —<u>and</u> the future! Without them there is just another soldier in green muddling his way through a war to an unknown future.

'Stelle, I hate to be magnanimous or noble but—well—don't let me get you down.—What only matters to me is that you and I—stick to the "friends." I never felt so much like a heel as I do now.—What in heaven's name do I have to offer you—a few years of anxious waiting—perhaps yes, perhaps no, then what??—Its not logical. Its not cricket. It doesn't make sense. My alleged unconcern for home is undoubtedly caused by extreme envy for those who can enjoy those things. Its unfair I know to be so selfish….One occasionally suffers from that self-pitying angle—Don't sympathize—just give me a boot….

We're okay, 'Stelle—we'll always be okay —We still think in the same way.—There is no barrier….

110

What I feel, think, do—all has to be professional, unemotional,——
'Stelle—You understand I'm sure….

I do care very much. Don't you see—if I were not to care there would
be nothing—rien. There are no others but you—and that's what makes me
so angry with myself—There you are the only thing I really love or care
about and I go ahead and cage you up in a cell—a jail with bars of a silly
ring—Love should be unselfish—Like a dog I dug a hole to hide my bone
from all others.

I can't truthfully say that I want you to forget it but—well—Use your
own judgement—The ring is not a pair of shackles—It's a symbol of my
esteem for you and a request that you keep me in mind.—Lets say I've got
an option.—Let's say that if you believe I won't fill my end of the deal or
that I'll be too late in paying up you can tear up the contract.—If you get a
handsome offer—a more satisfying agreement—go to it—

Me?—There's only one company I want to work for!!—

I still haven't got the guts to write that letter—You see me in [?]
soldiers—I see you in her— 'Stelle I'm not a coward—an escapist but
damn it—it's the company commanders job to write condolences!!—not
mine——Hah—what a laugh—what a ….

Kiss me darling, hold me close.

> Your
> Sid

Mar. 1
Darling—

… 'Stelle, in regards to that Japanese Wave course at U. of Colorado—
Its Mar. 1 now and by the time this gets to you it undoubtedly will be too
late but if you decided to go through with it—my heartiest congratulations.
True its hard to stomach anything associated with the Navy but from your
point of view and your future I do feel it would be wise. As you say—it has
definite post-war possibilities—

If you didn't—(which, by the way, is probably what happened)—no
difference—'Stelle you've got the stuff that'll put you on top whatever
you do!!—Don't quibble—its true!!—okay—you like radio, you like
writing—give it a push you've got nothing to lose—You like English,
acting, directing, plays—dig into it—

If your future looks so bleak and uncertain just put yourself in my
shoes. If nothing befalls me as a result of my "vocational hazards" what
then? Where do I go from there??—Tsk—Perhaps its this uncertainty
that's been transferred to you—us—us—

Oh–I can sleep in a hole, I can wash my clothes, sew buttons on my shirts. I could string barbed wire— "Any barbed wire today lady?" I can calculate fire data and direct fire so's I could hit a barn— "Want a barn knocked down, mister?" Shoot?—A qualified expert with the rifle—"Shoot your husband for you missus?" A jungle fighter. "Got any jungles?"—

My ridiculous plight is no worse than millions of others—Pray God the people at home have the decency to give us half a break when we return. Most soldiers are accustomed to taking advantage of the slightest opportunity—I'm sure the majority will take full cognizance of any benefits to be derived from these efforts.

Of course there is that damned pride of mine that will have to be contended with—

Well, why worry about that now—You know the facts—I can't change my affection for you—I suppose whatever emotion you feel towards me is fairly settled—If you still want this empty hulk when I return all it can do is try, try earnestly to live up to the faith you've shown in me—I will!—

All this "Sears" conversation is morale busting—or somethin'—I've seen enough of people, life, death, to know that out of what seems an unholy mess of confusion and doubt there usually comes a successful order and certainty.—All a matter of time—

By the by about that farther and further deal—...pliz pliz halp me... Angles is a funny lengwich—...

Ye Gods for an officer with half a grain (hm?) of intelligence I can write the most ridiculous, dull junk—Such is your fate—Engaged to a half wit. I say this only because I know this is one point we agree upon,— Something about He came, He saw, He concurred.

I love you—intensely

Your,
Sid

The following letter was written during a lull in the fighting. "O.P." means Observation Post.

Mar. 2
Darling, sweet!

So its incomprehensible that I might write 2 letters in one day!!— hm—Sometimes I love you just that much more—which is undoubtedly a powerful state.

I shall classify myself as a chronic paranoiac. Of all the selfish, self-pitying, fools I take the cake—Please, please don't take any of my previous drooling seriously—its not really true. Just a bit lonesome for you—a bit tired of the heat, nothing more. I always was and will be the optimist. That "everything will turn out satisfactorily" attitude.—Why I bother shedding my woes on your shoulder is beyond me. Perhaps its because I like your shoulder—I like you.—True, its good to blow off steam occasionally— healthy or something—but don't ever, ever, <u>ever</u> think that you and I—we,—us—has taken a secondary position in my thoughts—We'll be okay!—huh??—You let off your steam occasionally—I'll do likewise— only lets not go at it too long.

I want to make you happy—I don't want you thinking or worrying—If you're okay that's good enough for me.—

The way towards understanding women is a tough and grueling grind. I think I know you—The trouble is we're bound somehow—You feel despondent, uncertain—I feel the same—I get gay—you get gay— Whatever happens I know I've been tied to you by a knot mightier than the scrap of paper called marriage.—(Day after!!!)— 'Stelle that discomfort, restlessness is here too—Some would say its because I haven't seen a woman black or white in months— —but—somehow its only you I think about!!—Sweet I do love you—

So you wanted to study Japanese—Very interesting. True it would have its advantages but it has definite drawbacks. Every time you'd yell "Banzai" I'd stick a bayonet through you and it wouldn't look right—my being married to a sieve.

The day was spent climbing steep hills to O.P.'s where one could see for miles around—a truly striking view. Below stretched the green dark occult jungle. Preternatural mists hovered over the swamplands. Turning about one could see the ocean—the blue, quiet Pacific—seemingly growing from the lowlands tremendous hills towered in the distance— "No man's land." Given a choice I would not take you to a south sea island "Paradise"—That four room apartment in the Bronx looks awfully attractive from here—Please let me put my feet on your coffee table??— Please??...

Enclosed you will find a money order. It is not to buy your affections or to pay for the mortgage!—You will follow instructions implicitly or— well—you know me when I get mad!! (some threat oo-ha!!)

1. Take said blue stuff and change for green lucre.
2. Purchase one copy of Ogden Nash's "Good Intentions" and—read it—no—don't send it—I've read it—Just been tickled slightly by his "Poetic license" with a helluva lot of bootlegging on the side.—You'll see what I mean

3. Please—please go out and buy something which you've always wanted but have refrained from purchasing because—it wasn't practical—so be good—get something nice, different—It will make me happy—okay???—Then go out and have that good time—

4. Purchase a book for me—anything—your likes are mine—

5. Also send some colored pencils—soft—preferably "china marking pencils"—Red, blue, black—No—not the innate artiste coming out—good for marking maps and overlays—

6. Spend the rest foolishly...

I love you—darling—extensively—

> Your
> Sid

Oh—yes—also send some Garden seeds—In our spare time we occasionally get the urge to putter....Lets see—almost anything will grow down here except my hair—we'd like to get enough to perhaps give all of us a bite of fresh vegetables...

Ah yes—include, please, some instructions!—The only experience I've got in the realm of gardening is a pea plant in a shoe box which didn't grow—a tulip in the closet which my 3A teacher said was nice—an onion grown in a milk bottle. A fair background but hardly enough for this "plantation" stuff....

You see what you get for demanding that I ask you to get things. With an insatiable lust I keep asking for things and more things—Don't rush about 'em—

After a day in the heat, a shower and a letter from you make me feel like the richest man in the world. Gosh—if every man and woman doesn't envy me they don't appreciate value—I love you

> Your
> Sid

Mar. 3

To my darling,

'Stelle, you've become a veritable integral part of the days routine. After the "feast" of the evening and shower I settle down to writing and being near you. I love you so maddeningly its far from the "usual" boy, girl affair. It is different—I know. Interminably I'm plagued by some one's tale of woe. This one believes his wife's running around. He's frantic with distrust and imaginative fears. He talks of violent action such as divorce or cutting her off without a dime etc. Is it strange that never once have I felt uncertain?—Is it peculiar that if such nonsense should occur that I'd understand?? What is it about our relationship which seems to hurdle the pettiness of the rest?—You—You and your friendship—you and your trust—you and your devotion —It may sound fatuous to speak of ethereal joinings but you are a part of me—just as much as my arm.—Without it I could live—I could laugh—I could work—But there would always be something missing from the entity—certain comforts and operations of body and mind would be curtailed—Yes, it is possible to "get along" without an appendage – but how much more "whole" is the heart and soul with all its parts.

Go ahead—call me a sentimental "boggle boggle." "Sticks and stones etc."

Speaking of "spare parts" and vital necessities—How long does it take to get married in New York—three, four days??—too long—too long—We'll have to make a dash for Connecticut (if I could spell it) or something—what?—You won't be bullied??—Am I making threats? Am I proposing physical violence?—I only mention the fact that the kidnap vehicle will be handy with a crew of trusty "henchmen" to spirit you away. So they give you chloroform!—so they twitch your nose and make you say yes!—So my gremlins make you say "I do" when all the time you want to yell for help.—Can't you see—you're done for—surrounded—put up the white flag and I promise to beat you but once a week and help wipe the dishes—

A few more months out here in hades and I'll be capable of just that— Gr-rr-rr-rr!!!

By the by in order to allay any fears—I really do love you—very very much—

Your, Sid

Mar. 29
Darling,

I feel whoozy to the nth degree. Last night occasioned the luxury of twelve hours slumber. One gets that— "Oh how I hate to get up" feeling, but duty, chow, the birds all order— "Get the hell outta bed—soldier!"

We've brought our cots out to our holes and sleep is ever so much more enjoyable minus stumps, stones, rocks.

There's very little to report. Your soldier-boy is still "sans" injury.

You ask about any hand-to-hand fighting. The closest I've come to any fight occured a while ago. We were up in an O.P. cut into a large boulder

115

resting high atop a ridge.—Nippo attacked at night—Sitting high over it all, it was just like witnessing a fourth of July fireworks show from a grand stand seat. As the battle crept closer to us we all tightly clenched our carbines. A case of hand grenades was opened and distributed—We kept reporting the progress of the fray over the phone—Very similar to a blow-by-blow ringside description. In the morning Tojo started sniping and getting himself sent to his honorable ancestors.—But that was long ago.—

I'm getting more proficient in my work as time goes by—We've gotten several verbal commendations but the most pleasing of all is a remark from a front line infantryman.—The man that sits in his hole with no alternative but kill or be killed— "We sure were glad to have that mortar fire!"— 'Stelle—if I could do anything to help them—dig holes with my fingernails, I'd do it. They are gallant men.

No—I never did write that letter.—I have some courage—but not that much.

Remember Lt. Foster—my exec.—He's "purple hearting"—only a slight wound—A Lt. House has come to me for training—I hate these men with wives and kids—they don't belong here…

After the battle there was the usual souvenir hunt—Somehow I still have respect for the departed—couldn't get myself to pick up a battle flag or something—

So ends our gory tale of carnage, and carrion—…

By the way I still love you—very much—However I'm still in doubt as to whether I'll accept your leap year proposal if you make it.—Follow my "whim of the moment" as "some" people say—

Every time I go through a period of anxiety—I take it out on us—you particularly—don't take it seriously—Just a child getting cranky for lack of sleep. Okay?…

I love you darling—overwhelmingly—Please—please know that—Please, please understand—that—well there are times a guy's just not himself—You know what I mean. Or do you?—

> I love you
> Your
> Sid

March 30
Darling—

Take a look out in the park. Is the sun shining? Are the trees comfortably green? Do the birds sing and shout joyously? Is everything hushed but for the far away noises of living? Is it serene, peaceful, quiet?—Then—then darling you are sharing the present moments with me....

How content with the world one can be! Satisfied with nature's elegance. How sad it is that man must come to destroy, scar, and burn....But, like the siren of old she tires of the seduction of men and whips into the fury of rain, mud, darkness, green—rotten fungus—death—...Sometimes one thinks enduring all her violence is worthwhile as long as she unfolds her loveliness to us on these rare occasions of peace—

This is just like a Sunday at home. Last night there was ten hours of good sleep. A few articles read from the New Yorker (the only reading material I have up here)—loafing on cot.—Lt. House seated at the desk calculating fire data for support fire—Like doing his homework—...

Leap year sort of cramps a guy's style.—I can't cook a lamb chop for you or make "good" fried potatoes—Can't even invite you to tea—

Despite this I still feel like having you seated beside me—I'd just like to hold your hand and look dreamily at the wall—used to do it quite often with you—

Lets see—The bookcase of the Speros—The ridiculous clay busts—The sail boat that would never sail. That fascinating little samivar that made the funny noise when you banged the cup.—The "bishop"— or "friar" with his fat jovial mien.—The painting—no—lets see—there used to be a painting, then you took the small photographs of your grandparents from the right side and hung them there.—The coffee table —How I feared it!—I was so sure I'd break it or scratch it with my wonted clumsiness.—...The two lamps on either side of the couch that had the hidden switches that one could never find.—The bright reflector light I hated so much—The two wall lights—one never did work.—The idol of the Speros—to which one bowed and scraped reverently—the mighty, omnipresent, omniscient potentate—the "piano." He who would dain to touch it kindled the wrath of the Gods! (both of 'em) —The rug that made electricity on a dry day...The door with the white curtain.—The chair which always threatened to cave in but never did —The lounging chair —The fake flowers on the piano—How I wanted to keep it filled with live ones.

You see darling —You and I are not so far apart—

I'm there now—Gone is the musty odor of an underground hole—Gone are the sand walls—In my reverie—I am with you—near you—close to you—

How I do love you!!—...

Be good—Have fun—don't—don't be lonely—Live as full a life as possible—...

I am—
Your
Sid

Sid's parents lived in a street-level apartment, a portion of which they had turned into a small neighborhood dress shop. His mother had told me about the incident described below in Sid's letter, and I had teased Sid about it. This letter was his response to my teasing. (Parksville was the town where Sid had worked as a waiter one summer.)

Mar. 31
Darling,

Dilemma! Confusion! Distraction!! – My past returns to haunt me—skeletons rattle their bones in my closet. Once more the Nelson Dress Shoppe is my undoing—

So a girl from Coney Island walks in to buy a dress. She spots my sorry puss hanging from the wall – She swoons and shrieks in terror – "Is that—is that-that Monster Sidney Diamond"—(It must have happened this way)—So my picture leers back at her and says, "What's it to ya bub?"—

"Sure," she says, "I knew him in Parksville—He used to call me fat and when I was sick with appendicitis he sent me a lollypop —"—"Evelyn something or other's my name," she states—

Nights of tossing and turning. Who the hell is Evelyn—I've called a lot 've 'em fat –(Candid Sid)—The lollypops—oh—oh —oh—It hit me like a flash—

It was one of those Irv (Charlie) Jacobson, Phil, Diamond screwy escapades.

Some guy writes a book "Out of the Night"—Mine's "Out of the Nelson"—Some say that if you stand on Broadway and 42nd St., you'll meet someone you know—the Nelson apparently has taken over some of the work – all of my "lurid" past parades before that photo on the wall – Ah yes – I shall drink me a bottle of the "Green Death" and retire to the ignominious hovel –

She says she took pictures of us – Yoiks, they hitched the five miles from town and grabbed us for the pictures before we knew what was going on—Women are crazy—insane—and should be watched carefully—

A guy can't get engaged in peace—

I fully expect a bare breasted native girl in a sarong to walk into the Nelson—glance at the photo—and shout— "Uggle bub—sut phlub—Heel—me him see 'em—no good Joe—Double bubble—rubble!"

What a life! What a world!!— damn I could make a good strategist for this war —I read all the funnies—to quote a rotten gag in a rotten paper—

For you—alone—a very fond caress—a kiss—because—just because—

Your
Sid—

119

Bougainville, April 1944

April 11 was Sid's birthday, his 22nd—and almost exactly 2 years since he had arrived at Fort Dix after enlisting.

April 11

Darling,

Today is my birthday. Frankly I feel one hundred years older. How was this auspicious anniversary celebrated?—Alone with the fruit cake you sent. Imagine—I received it on my birthday and am having my own private party—Yum!!

As I sit here slowly masticating the heavenly cake I can't help sympathize with you at home. You have never experienced the tingling joy of a fruit cake after months of army chow—and a good deal of it "C" rations. Could you possibly comprehend the sheer ecstacy of slowly rolling the raisins over your dentures? The extreme delight of playing with the cherries—swooshing them back and forth—is overwhelming. Ah, the kindness of the Gods blesses you with a walnut!! This is the zenith of pleasure!! I have lived and experienced all the joys of heaven—Ah the glorious walnut!—Can anything surpass the teasing taste of the rum. The Juarez Cuba Libras could never match this—this nectar—ambrosia—

Frankly, darling, I doubt whether I've ever enjoyed a birthday so much. I have the newly arrived "New Yorker," your fruit cake, a sense of humor, and still comparatively slug-nutty. I am alone—no strain—no tension—at peace with all....

Ah yes—I love you—very dearly, tenderly. Gosh how I miss you!!! Your photograph is now being nicely framed in mahogany by our company artisan. Frankly, I can't see how a beautiful girl like you sees anything in this sorry excuse for a bread-getter—Such are the follies of youth.—

Darling, I do love you

Your

Sid

April 16

Darling,

No mail from you to me. Sad, sad, dreary day. The days are completely devoid of any activity. The main topic of conversation is this new "rotation" policy whereby men with 18 mos. to 2 yrs. overseas will get an opportunity to go home. We've got a long time before we fulfill the requirements but it gives a man hope! Its good to know that eventually one may get another short glimpse of the bright lights and apartment houses. Once more, perhaps, to shave with hot water, to have wood for a floor, a leak proof

roof.—…But, as usual, it's a daydream born of too much leisure, Frankly, once you've been in action you acquire a peculiar philosophy. It sounds something like this. If I get it, okay!—If I don't get it—okay!…

Ye Gods one would think that being to the rear would allow a fellow some rest.

No deal—we start our artillery barrages early—almost rolls you out of bed when the big boys start shouting. One just curses, remembers the times he was on the receiving end and whispers Give 'em hell!—Then one tries desperately to sleep.!

These Solomons are definitely places lend-leased from Hell—Speaking of lend-lease please be informed that it does not include fiancées to Canadians or others—Frankly, I'm jealous—now darn it don't tell me I'm not—you always talk me out of these things. I'm in a very obdurate mood—if I say I'm envious—I am—so there!—and will you please send me another fruit cake before I really lose my temper—woof!

Sweetheart—darling—I love you, want you, need you—

> Your
>
> Sid
>
> Your very own!

In spite of what he had been through, Sid's humor had not been crushed, nor had his love.

April 17, 1944

Now I know our future. We're going into the shoe business! When I gaze at my tremendous array of shoes I shudder! First we have my good old <u>G</u>overnment <u>I</u>ssue field shoes, two pair. Then, flopping forlornly by them are my jungle calf high sneakers—guaranteed to protect from mosquitoes, bugs, ants and to keep you from being heard by the enemy. You'd love them. They're green (supposedly for camouflage). I've worn them once and went back to my leather G.I.'s.— Next we have the knee high rubber boots, good only for rear areas where one wears fancy clothes and is particular about getting one's feet wet. The fancy dress oxfords purchased when I received my commission lie dejected, molding, dull! Remember how they clicked so arrogantly and proudly. They caused no end of chagrin on the dance floor.

Recently my parents sent a pair of moccasins. There was the usual delay in delivery. They grew panicky—afraid their son would pass away if he didn't get these comforts—So they sent another pair, more expensive, more "beautiful." Now I have two such luxuries. I tremble when I think of moving. I'll need several 2 1/2 ton trucks, jeeps, porters, stevedores to get my impedimentia wherever we go. Ah yes—what—what a life!—

I don't want to be insulting but do you think perhaps you could wear a shoe size 9 1/2E?—huh?—Then we could save on shoe expenses....

Seriously, sweetheart—a year ago I presented you with a token, a talisman. It was given in appreciation of a grand friend, comrade, sweetheart—in the fond hope that eventually we, you and I, could spend the rest of our lives together, driving each other crazy.—I said then and repeat with a sincerity unchanged—I love you!!—Through the turmoil and strife, when I cried with fear my first night in battle—there was always you and your heckling to make me laugh, to bring me back to normal. When I returned from the front with the nauseating stench of the dead lingering on my clothes it was the memory of the past, which is you, that made me throw off the melancholy of the moment. I don't know when I'll return. I don't know whether or not you'll still want me—But for your loyalty and warm affection I'm deeply and humbly thankful—I repeat—Thanks for being the best a guy ever had—...

I love you.
Your
Sid

In his desire to spare me anxiety, Sid wrote little about what he faced in battle. But there were times when he had to.

April 21
Darling,

The birds sing, the air is cool, everything is pleasant—at long last—a letter—nay two letters from my fair regina.—

Lets see—yours of April 8th. What did I do on Passover?—I participated in a push—nothing spectacular—Just did my job. You speak of my seeming displeasure. That my letters sound as if something is wrong.—Have you ever seen a dead body –a torn twisted, confused mess?—Not one, two but great masses?—Have you ever spent a day with the stench of carrion??—Did you ever stand hypnotized by the whirring flies as they mingled with the confusion that once was a man—even if he was a Jap?—

Something was definitely wrong!! Please, darling, don't—don't try and put all my stupid reactions on your own very pretty shoulders. There's nothing wrong between us. If anybody needs the kick and the bawling out its your fiancé (1 "e") who's a damn idiot anyway—

Now look, sweetheart (I am now frowning and trying to look stern!)—we'll have none of this "going to school may be by passed. What's the difference what happens." Its important to you and me!! You must do everything you ever dreamed or hoped to do. I want you to—sincerely. True, I can't guarantee to be of much assistance. Can't you see, sweet, both of us can't be frustrated! One of us must continue—you are what makes this "us."—This all sounds very confusing but I feel very confused—Whatta war—whatta war—whatta damn war!!

Now we are confronted with your letter of the 11th. My dear darling only one its not fair to delve into a mans past, particularly when that mans past involves a buster brown haircut—My God who dug that up? I recall the photograph. There rode gallant sonny boy on his white charger with his underwear sticking out from beneath his shorts. Wait, wait—I'll get your mother to show me some of your "better" photographs.—Then you'll feel sorry. Boy, you must've been an ugly kid—all that beauty couldn't possibly have been with you all your life—there must've been some moments when you weren't attractive…

Sweetheart, I haven't changed too much. I'm still your guy. I can't see myself anywhere else but with you. How I wish I could make you understand how meaningless are those periodic stages of coldness.—'Stelle, try, try hard to comprehend that I've been away for so long, that I grow lonely, that when I need and want you most I cover my weakness with a veneer of perhaps—lets say "peculiar" attitudes. 'Stelle I can't bring myself to burden you with the unhappy moments….Be good, will you—let'em pass. For heaven's sake don't think its your fault….

Lord, all this writing and I haven't told you I love you as yet—consider yourself very much adored, accept a kiss, and no back talk!

> Your
>
> Sid

Peter Ibbetson, (as mentioned before in these headnotes), was a play in which separated lovers arrange to meet in their dreams.

April 21, 1944
Friday 8 P.M.
Darling,

I've just completed a letter to you. Somehow I feel so close to you now that its impossible to drag myself away so I begin another one to prevent the continuity, the nearness from being disturbed.

How peculiar, I can't stop. What's going on? I feel you here beside me!!   What were you doing at about 0200 A.M. April 20? Thursday?— Could you too have been thinking of me. 'Stelle this is uncanny. You're standing next to me. Darling, I feel your warmth. There is the odor of fresh clean soap you usually carry with you. 'Stelle this is bad—I musn't—Either I'm going bats or somethings peculiar. Stop playing Peter Ibbetson!— Sweetheart if only you were real, if only I could hold your hand, look into your eyes, kiss you—-

'Stelle——I better stop.

Your
Sid

The skepticism, verging on cynicism, expressed in this letter was quite unusual for Sid.

April 24

My little virago—

Darling today has been a bleak weary day. The interminable rainy season apparently has engulfed us once more. Day, after day, after day it rains. Living has become one endless mud puddle. To increase the unpleasantness of the whole universe we were not blessed by a letter from the very much adored sweetheart....

I've completed "Candide," Voltaire's little contribution to the confusion of man. Ah yes, everyone through the ages has condemned the iniquities of the human race. 'Tis easy enough to play upon the obvious. And what does he offer as the solution? "Eldorado" the utopia in South America. So Christ offered the "hereafter," Marx was to smash the chains of the proletariat, Hitler was to give the Germans and the world a "new order," Roosevelt wanted a "New Deal," Hirohito gave his people the "Japanese Destiny." 'Stelle, everybody offers an imaginary and unattainable "Eldorado."— Maybe I'm wrong but somebody's got to show me a "good" community way of life. Move over, sister, I'm joining the league of cynics!—

My darling, tenderness and sugared words are a bit out of my line, but sweet knowing you has made these past years a dream of happy companionship and affection. Even though you do have a red nose and impale me weekly I believe I could spend the rest of my life letting you make me happy. As for me—no looks, no money, no personality—all I offer is my dogged devotion and respect....

'Stelle, again and again I repeat my gratitude for this Coleman lantern. Believe me, sweet if there was any inconvenience on your part, it has brought boundless pleasure to your guy and has, therefore, I hope repaid you in some small way. Frankly you make me swell with pride—You're a—a—peach!

> I love you,
> Your,
> Sid

Sid was never out of my thoughts. I felt a new moodiness in his letters that indicated emotional hazards outside of battle.

April 26, 1944
Darling,

You are perfectly correct in dressing me down for my recent outrageous moods. Perhaps if I explained the tales of woe that add to one's tenseness and uncertainty.

My men... are continually harassed by sweethearts marrying. Of course, that's to be expected. After all there was no bond. That doesn't bother so much but when wives take off and start forgetting their husbands that's bad. Then there's the case where a man's wife writes she's expecting a little bundle of joy. Ah yes—marriage by proxy, children the same way—Ugh!

The one I like best is the story of one of my former sergeants. He was engaged and even went so far as to purchase a bedroom set. She gets married and now the happy couple are using his bed——He swears to burn the bed from under them!—

I believe you can understand how a guy feels. You sort of become enraged at the whole situation and deep inside there grows a gnawing and aggravating doubt. "You've been a lucky devil—so far. This may happen to you—no—yes—no"—A man feels so helpless down here so far away from everything. I realize such a thing is quite normal and very possible—but believe me I don't want it that way. All teasing and joking aside you are the "one and only."—During all the years I've known you there's never been a one that could make me disloyal in thought or action—Darn it kid you've been my sweetheart from the first time I walked you home from the handball court.

'Stelle no one realizes more thoroughly what I lost when I left than me, no one feels more strongly the unhappiness and loneliness you may have experienced for, so help me—I've had it twicefold.

Look, when things get rough—even after this mess—promise never to take any of my sarcastic moods seriously—okay—and I'll try desperately

to keep my equilibrium. I want so much not to hurt you in any way——
Well—I just want you to keep on thinking of me as your guy——

You scarcely realize how powerful and overwhelming your hold
is upon me. You've been sister, cousin, friend, sweetheart, fiancée all
wrapped in one…

I am now reading "The Making of the Mind"….there's a difference
between being smart and intelligent.—What's the difference??—Well—
Supposin' I was to kiss you and make up every time you buy a new hat—
that's smart—When I break your arm and spank you soundly—that's
intelligent! …

> Sweet—I love you
> Your,
> Sid

*While I was looking forward to starting graduate studies in theatre
at Northwestern University, Sid was at a field hospital awaiting spinal
surgery for a cyst. He was to be in the hospital for more than a month, a
good deal of the time spent lying perfectly still on his side.*

*"Pink evenings" referred to in this letter was our sobriquet for
evenings of intellectual, or at least, intelligent discussion.*

May 23
Darling,

Look, in order not to break the continuity of mail how about your
new address at Wisconsin, Northwestern, Kalamazoo or wherever you
finally decide to attend. Today, this very evening Sidney – Lt. Sidney
N.M.I. Diamond received not one but two letters from a certain swell
personality…

'Stelle, there must definitely be a patron saint, lady luck or something
hovering over me. You see they don't do elective surgery in line hospitals
so the plan was to evacuate me down the line to a general hospital. Well
I wasn't interested in being separated from my outfit so the doctor and
I hemmed and hawed, made investigations and finally got around the
ruling by calling it an acute case needing immediate surgery.—Had I been
evacuated I would have left on a certain morning on a particular plane.—
Well—I learned later that everyone back at camp thought I was finished,
caput, lost, "demised"—the plane—well it just—well—lets say "it doesn't
live here anymore"—I was supposed to be aboard!!—More things happen
or nearly happen to me than is comfortable….

I'm very elated over those school offers. I'm very proud—...You know how I feel—I'm on your team. You just made another goal for old alma mater....

When are we going to have pink evenings??—That's hard to say—first thing I'm going to do is kiss you—say Hello—kiss you again—then just walk—holding your hand—I don't want to talk—don't want to embrace you — just walk—feeling you beside me —...As for the pink evenings—give me time—not too much—but I do so hate to talk over my head—don't you understand—I must catch up—I must know!—I must regain confidence in my ability to talk and act like a civilian—

Two years is a long time—longer than most people can imagine—two years of harshness of brutality of coarseness—I have to get out of the habit of talking with a note of finality.— 'Stelle there's so many things—it frightens me to think of it—

Well—that's in the future—I love you

Your
Sid

May 27

Darling,

Today has been conspicuous for its complete lack of any writeable activity and the pleasure of four letters from you. Answering those letters will be the problem of the day.

Before we start you must comprehend the confusion in the mail situation. You see I've already received and answered letters of the 12th and 13th and now I'm faced with yours of the 6th and 8th. – Well "here goes" he said as he dived from the Empire State building— "Here goes nothing!"

May 8th Sweetheart in regard to those "expert" fetishes. I possess an "expert" in rifle marksmanship and Chemical Warfare weapons—Got those way back at Bliss....

May 6 "After we're married I expect you to be bored green—and there won't be another island to look forward to!" Thank God 'Stelle I'll be able to forget every bit—every single bit about these islands and my war experiences. Its only by constant movement that one can keep from thinking—and that's what I want to do.—And don't you sh-sh —I want to be with you—all the time—me!!!!...

The bracelet—oh—it'll survive—I wouldn't part with it for anything in the world....it was with me during my first action and I sorta want it around. You see before going into combat you usually leave your valuables behind. I seriously considered leaving your ring and bracelet—then I decided I wasn't going to get hurt so that was that.—One night the poor enlisted man sharing my hole on the line kept waking me up every time my hand came out of my pocket—the flash of the ring or bracelet might expose our position to Tojo who was playing around outside our wire. The audacious little nit wits even lit a flash once to draw fire.—

May 16 The typewritten one!... 'Stelle— — 'Stelle—really I don't like to sound like an overemotional jackass. Perhaps you should know, you are part of me—The bugles stopped blowing a long time ago. Sir Arthur and Sir Galahad have been burned out of me—I'm a mediocre officer at best but I do my job—I get a salary—I save a little which may help after its over—After my two years in the God Damned Tropics perhaps I'll go home—Maybe I'll be successful, maybe I won't but 'Stelle this is one hombre that cares little for people—...

'Stelle there's going to be so many oh so many problems. So many difficulties—...oh—nuts—just lets love each other and let the rest of the world go to the devil—huh?

I am your
Sid

Back again. I had a good night's rest and feel perfectly normal and rational....

Perhaps if people could be instructed away from mass thinking—one mass hating another mass—If we can get each person to settle his private grievance without calling in his family, his race, his country to assist....It's a hopeless confusion. We all seek escape to Eldorado. You and I would like to just hide together...We want to be left alone—

Say—what the devil—stop me—I'm going in circles—not arriving at any definite conclusions—not generating any recommendations—Criticism is easy—What to do about it is another—

The biggest problem here in Ward 40 is how in heaven's name can we get rid of Frank Sin-Ah-Tra. We have no lights at night. Therefore we spend the evenings listening to the radio. Every time "Franky" comes on there's a universal groan—heads bury themselves under pillows—The cries of pain are pitiful...

Oh—today I received a May 15th issue of "Time"!! They send the "pony edition" direct from Honolulu. Its devoid of advertisements and unnecessaries and is small enough to fit in the ordinary business envelope....

Concerning that expert hardware—never wore 'em. If I could get out of wearing the campaign ribbons I'd like nothing better—not false modesty just don't like people asking me what they're for and then having to go into long stories....

I love you—Your Sid

The intense emotion aroused by D-Day was felt in the hospital.

June 7

The news of the continental invasion is the primary source of conversation. You probably have had yourself stuffed with the news etc. consequently we need not go into it — I heard the report during a movie in the hospital — Picture was stopped—news announced—'Stelle—there were no cheers—no shouts—we all sat still—We'd fought—we'd made beach heads — — Ours was a deep sympathy –a silent prayer—"Good Luck, brother, — good luck!!"

One of Sid's fraternity brothers wrote that he was anxious to get overseas and "to play a more vital role." Sid wrote to me: "All faintly reminiscent of a guy named Sid two years ago—only Sid now has grown very old—His youthful exuberance has been milked by almost a year in the tropics—He's very tired of crusades—He reads the news now and chuckles—Another year down here and he'll probably die laughing. He knows humans can't change—you can't satisfy 'em—rich, poor, educated, uneducated, intelligent, moronic—all have that streak which makes for greed— —One might as well succumb to these traits and fight so that you can have more — more — more — !!!

'Stelle—its that I believe wholeheartedly in the way of government we have—I know how corrupt some of it is—I know it doesn't function smoothly but I believe it can be made to operate successfully—"

(The first part of this letter was typed, with dots instead of Sid's usual dashes)
June 19
Darling,

Now, after exactly 33 days in the hospital they have finally released me...

The package containing the reams of paper has just arrived. Whats the use of saying thanks. You couldn't possibly comprehend the gratitude and love I feel. I am looking forward to the pleasant moments reading those books. Its most disconcerting however..... First I fondle the page—Like a child my eyes goggle at the smooth shiny new pages — There's something about a new book that affects me that way........

"This book is mine....I own it......It is unsoiled. No dull inappreciative hands have mauled its pages....it has come to me from someone.....

The book is not mine its ours....The words contained within it tell of experiences, thoughts, emotions....That person and I through this strange medium can share the adventure, the enjoyment.....Is it not similar to an evening together at a movie?....Can we not laugh together think together as at a lecture?....Are we not united by the text?....Is it not a date?

And I'll have vanilla.

Heck, sister, once I get back under your wing wild horses couldn't drag me away— You're going to get awfully tired of this wither thou goest — but all wanderlusting post-bellum—will be done by us, together, simultaneously, at the same time!

I read with interest your statement about the individual—completely and objectively studying his reactions—Remember a long long time ago we thought of a plot for a play in which the hero was isolated from the world and then a study of his reactions when he encounters other people. Remember?...

'Stelle the only way we can get a true insight into what we should be is to create a child — an ectogenic production — They have made cells grow and multiply, glands have been fed and kept alive and pulsating—Why is it not possible by mixing the proper ingredients, correct temperature, minute and careful feeding—to create a human—The creation would be free of the prejudices of man—He would be the "control.",...We have no fear of hereditary traits — gullibility, excitability etc. could never be attributed to some mythical parent — He would have no race—Will he need friendship? Will he feel the need to travel with the crowd? Does the mind need something like astrology or religion?—Will he envy? Will he hate?—Will he fight for food? Will he also fight for a belief? Will he sense right and wrong?

Then of course he must be educated—what to teach him? — Say we stuff him with nothing but facts—Will he draw "intelligent" conclusions without influence?

The purpose of all this?—To find out definitely whether its worthwhile attempting to change people—Maybe the "control" will prove that a "construction" consisting of a bone framework, two legs, two arms, eyes, ears, so many ounces of gray matter material—fed by so many calories, vitamins, protein etc.—cannot exist happily without hate, bigotry, stupidity, violence — Maybe man is not meant to be "intelligent" —...And so on into the night — ...

Last night we had a long discussion on religion and intermarriage between religions...The final conclusion arrived at is that two people of "intelligence" can adjust themselves but in case of children one of the two must consent to sacrifice his religion and let the children be brought up one way...

Tonight there will be a discussion "on the values of being faithful or faithless to your wife" It should prove "interesting" — and I will not make a report —

This is a very long bit of nothing. All I really wanted to say was—I love you — very much

Your
Sid

In June a friend of Sid's gave a party to cover up the pain of a "dear John" letter, and Sid was teased about what would happen to me at Northwestern University.

June 23

Darling,

Life is "tolerable." We are doing little else besides train and train some more. I'm going irrevocably mad trying to sell war bonds, inspire men to vote and unravel the spider web income tax regulations. Which reminds me—I didn't file a report for last year and am now being sought by the Treasury Department, F.B.I., Mayor LaGuardia and the O.S.C.

The big event of the week was a small party Lt. Rubin gave at his tent. You'll recall he's the chap who received the "I hope we'll remain friends" epistle from his fiancée who became engaged to some one else. So—oo—oo— we celebrated her marriage—killed a bottle of scotch—laughed—joked—all very jovial—Rubin was quite flushed—The boy she married was rich so we wished her luck—toasted the happy couple and talked some more.——

Of course, you entered the conversation after awhile—what would I do in the same situation. Practically the same as Rubin, I suppose—, shrug my shoulders—throw a bust – and hope that the gang wouldn't talk about her anymore —

When I told them you were going to Northwestern there were howls—two army forts, naval training center, big town, nightclubs in Chicago — — I was a "goner" as far as they were concerned—I replied with the usual and very appropriate "pass the peanuts please."

I'm giving a housewarming party tonight. You see I've received several packages, including your fruit cake. It is customary to occasionally invite the other officers over to the tent for an evening of beer, coca cola — peanuts — cake — cookies—— My tent has just been completed hence the joyous occasion. 'Stelle its really not a tent it's a small bungalow — a wooden floor, wood frame — canvas top — I even have a porch —!! Because of rank and so on I live in a tent by myself — usually they double up officers — (also because there was no other tent but a wall tent available) — Its very cozy—

Since my home lacks chairs, a table or glasses I'm giving the party in Rubin's and House's tent .

Finally received a letter from Herb B.—He's down in my neck of the Pacific—You'll never guess who else wrote—George M. H.—Lt. Junior grade U.S. Navy also somewhere in the Pacific. He wants to know if I'm married and if the unfortunate gal was 'Stelle—So I set him straight on a few of the details. Also had to give Len K. some fatherly advice about the feminine angle if he expects to get a nice girl — (well – that's not too important) just any gal that'll be willing to write more than once a month and who will appreciate the line of bull that all soldiers have — He's quite set on a babe in Petaluma, CA – Ah — love!

Two copies of In Fact lie on my "to be read" pile — occasionally stuff piles up so I have three stacks on my shelf — "to be read" "read" and "neuter"—

I've got a date with some Company Fund books and vouchers — Inspector General found a few irregularities so out I go getting initials etc. We got called down for not closing the account precisely on the last day of the month and not numbering pages and various like "important" matters.

Sweet—- Do you know that I love you — very very much???—

> And am very much
> Your
> Sid

There were now opportunities for recreation. "NAM" referred to in the following letter stood for National Association of Manufacturers.

June 24
Darling,

…My house warming was successful. We just gathered, ate fruit cake, cookies, almonds and sipped nectar of Satan and talked. There never was a lull in the conversation. The discussion ranged from Politics to the houses of prostitution in New Orleans—Why New Orleans is still a puzzle to all of us.

This has all the makings of being a very uninteresting and dreary letter…

My melancholy moment undoubtedly stems from the loss of a fountain pen and a cigarette lighter. Will my Chicago representative please purchase same and send to the wilds of the Pacific? All right all right so I'll make a formal request.

Dear Postman,
You look like a very happy man. You probably come from a happy home. Yes, your wife probably loves you—I love you—this girl admires you—We all have an affection for you—so please allow this lady—no you dope not the one on the left—the good looker in front of you—allow her to send me a pen—cigarette lighter—and a kiss——Hey!—in the letter!—in the letter!—Tend to your own business and sell stamps!!…

All is quiet here. Nearby a radio blurts out its unintelligible news reports. A whistle blows occasionally at a basketball game—A Negro team is playing our team—It's a pleasure to see the gallery—black and white—It looks like a good game—

This overseas service has been a great leveler—How pitiful it is that upon their return these boys will find conditions unchanged.—We have a radio station on the island that gives us transcriptions of the best <u>and</u> the worst the states have to offer.—Every Saturday a Jewish chaplain conducts a Sabbath service for a half hour over the radio.— Our biggest problem as officers is the orientation lectures. Three hours a week are devoted to discussion of the news. Officers are not permitted to deviate from facts or try to influence their men (which is good)—We glean our information from whatever sources available—Take a lecture I gave recently—a resume of the war situation—then a short talk on South America—and our problems there. We've taken up the racial question—We've gone through the party platforms of the coming elections—Labor vs. Capital—Unions vs. NAM—All have been covered—Then the facts—for both sides—In a hope that it would lead to more intelligent discussion by the men in their spare time—True a great many are more versed in this stuff than I or the other officers could hope to be but well—we try to get at all—The army's policy is to have the best informed soldiers in the world—

And what're you doin' Friday night?—Say I call for you about 10 P.M.—a short visit—Just to kiss you and say good night—sweet!

Your

Sid

Sid had been intent on sending me a bouquet of roses for my birthday, June 12, and I protested that under his present circumstances, it was not necessary for him to do this. (He did finally succeed.)

June 28

…My dear sweet 'Stelle I have no intention of keeping you in flowers as you grow older. I assure you that the only future you can expect with me is constant beatings, — endless harsh words — and almost complete neglect. Keep you in flowers indeed!! — It would be cheaper to marry you (I wonder) — Will you? — Will you what?? Stop asking silly questions— just say "yes" and trust Sidney. What dear? – You can't say the word Y— E — S? –You're telling me!! — Look — start like you're saying yoo—hoo but then stop at the oo—hoo — There — that's good! Now make like a lamb—e-e-ee-ee only stop at the e— Then join the ya and e-e and make it plural — that's it — that's it! Go on — y—e-e-e-s-sss! See! You could say it after all.

I'm pretty disgusted with this town Evanston you're at. I wrote to the Evanston Chamber of Commerce asking for the address of a florist. No reply!! What kind of business is that — And me a potential cash customer.— This is awkward. Is there a florist near your abode? Will he deliver the smelly stuff upon receipt of a money order? Or do I have to appeal to the red cross and say I must send flowers to a dead fifth cousin in Evanston who would really appreciate my thoughtfulness.—

My splurge into the field of agronomy is getting along nicely. I have my own little garden in rear of my tent. Already there are little tufts of green stuff coming from the soil. I feel so—so—earthy!—…At present I'm seriously worrying about the future of my little radishes and beans.— How to fertilize them? Strange as it may seem that can become a major problem. Why in our tomatoes section we had a great deal of difficulty getting the buds to become tomatoes. The same story "advanced mothers" tell their children when they ask "Where did we come from Mommie??" — Pollen—but no carrier—no medium—Our poor plants—impotent because no bees or bugs would carry the pollen. So-oo—we began "pimping" for our plants. — We'd launch a bit of dust off one bud and rub it on another…. They apparently survived because we did get a fine crop of nice luscious red tomatoes —All four of them!!! Now our happy home has been blessed by two bees who happily jump from one bud to another shooting the arrows of love into their very hearts. — Bigger and better tomatoes are expected. I am seriously considering settling some sharecroppers on my "farm" to attend to the "carrot row"!

Tonight I went to motion picture—"See Here Private Hargrove" – entertaining!   Sweet—Somehow I feel embarrassed when the end of the letter comes. Really—I do want to say the stuff and nonsense I feel — but supposing it sounds like so much drivel? — Without the flowery nonsense, without the roses, gardenias, engagement ring— the pretty words — I simply miss you. — Its strange I suppose — that a guy can just – "miss" something. Just like I've been accustomed to it my entire life….Lets just say quietly—gently—I love you.

Your

Sid

Summer classes at Northwestern had just begun.

July 1

…Your sensations upon going back to school—The problem always puzzled me from a subjective point of view. Its going into the third year now since I cracked a text book. Oh well—such is stuff.

This guy from U. of Ariz.—Hr-umph!!

I don't think I'll tell the gang about this one—It was bad enough when they had you going with a B.M.T. railroad engineer.— Just out of curiosity I might try.—The New Yorker always came in handy in that respect. They'd get it after me—find out the bands and stars playing at the Copacabana and have fun — at your expense…

Sweet, I fully comprehend that sudden loneliness [of] being away from the "old room" and its various memories. 'Stelle—you too must feel that gnawing inside—Like you're hungry only you've just eaten— A peculiar numb feeling inside—A desire to gush—only stubborn pride keeps you from emoting—You want company—so badly—You're seized with claustrophobia—You want to do something only you don't know what.

I never wanted to be with you more than now. Write and tell me about the place. So—it's a year—Very long time—I'm sure you'll make the most of it — Know and be sure that I'm your guy—I love you—and I think you're the best. —

And—How in tarnation do you come off scolding me for writing to Illinois—If I had the patience I'd bother to dig up you're letters…I'm abused!! All the time!! – Some men have nice polite young ladies that are quiet and patient and understanding –Me? …Our home will have three dog houses—I'm sure you'll drive me from one to the other — Also crazy.

136

I love you for your scolding—If you didn't find something wrong with me daily I'd begin to worry. — Not that there isn't something radically wrong with me daily — most noticeable is being away from you. —

Your

Sid

Here is an "interesting and true story" told to Sid by Lt. Rubin.

Rubin had been bathing in a shallow jungle stream near some infantry soldiers. As usual amongst soldiers they began talking of the merits of their own units when Rubin remarked that he was connected with the 4.2 mortars.

"Great gun," said a small G.I. "I had a funny experience—a lucky one—with one of your men.

It was the night of the Jap attack—They were pulling their god damned infiltration tactics on us. The whole line was jumpy as all hell. We were shootin' at frogs, rustlin' leaves or even nothin'—We all stayed in our holes—Anybody movin' out there was to be shot—

I'm on a big rock on top of hill X. From the top o' de rock you could see the whole line—We used it as an infantry O.P.—

It seems they sent one of your observers up to this O.P. after dark—only we didn't know he was comin'!! Suddenly I hears a noise— Somebody's climbin' up in the night.—I was too scared to challenge for the countersign—I raised my rifle — He was silhouetted against the skyline— a perfect target—I lined my front sight up with the battle sight—His head, the front sight, the rear sight were all in line—The shell was in the chamber—slowly I drew my breath—held it—Then I squeezed my trigger finger—slowly—slowly—I squeezed—Then my shoulder unconsciously tensed to meet the explosion — Click!!! — It didn't go off — a faulty cartridge — Brother some careless inspector saved that boys life!! —

Do you have a Lt. Diamond in your outfit??"

Sid's sketch in ink of his "Home Sweet Home!!" with a chair out front was included with this letter.

Darling,

Arise my love and come and live with me! — The above is my abode. Shanty? Ramshackle?? — Its very neat and clean and you only get wet when it rains hard. Not only has it Southern exposure but North, East, and West. In the rear grows a beautiful garden of Lima beans. We have cold running water from a shower nearby and the "maid" calls for you at 06:30 every morning except Sunday. With the home comes that easy chair depicted in the "painting"—There is no extra charge and that chair alone is worth three of the old fashioned type houses. The rooms, all one of them, are screened in. This screening, however, does not cause our love of nature's creatures to be stifled—for all sorts of lizards, ants and God's little children come to visit you through the cracks in the floor. The furnishings surpass "Spears" of New York. A voluptuous bed—mid-victorian in design, complete with overhead curtain. For those things usually thrown on the floor there are several nails attached to the walls to give it that modernistic touch. The Coleman Lantern Company guarantees light as long as you pay your bills and can steal white gas. There is a desk and soap box stool for those letter writing times. We have a shelf for underwear and books—those things closest to you — — a rack to hang clothes — The hangers are home made and the resulting creases and wrinkles gives one that "slumming" sensation. There is a large wastepaper basket which is also useful for the disposal of apple cores, match sticks, gum wrappers, and old copies of the OshKosh Herald. We will say no more — If interested apply to Sidney Diamond—

realtor and prospective spouse extraordinaire! Get your request in early — These homes are limited in number and already strange officers have been eyeing the screening covetously —...

This afternoon I did something which is bad—very bad for people down here—I just lay on my cot thinking and dreaming, seeing you and home and your parlor and Undercliff, and walks, and Highbridge, and plays, and dates, and carnivals, and fraternity houses, and rides in horse and carriage, and poetry recitals and us — and school, and friends. Just thinking back, letting my memory have free rein — Three full hours of that stuff is good for the soul but bad for the mind.

I love you—very much—and—well—23/4 hours this afternoon was devoted to you so it can't be too bad—I love you—

Your
Sid

The "Taylor" referred to below was my lovely roommate Jean Taylor.

July 5
Darling,

...I'm in an ugly mood tonight—a very ugly mood—Nothing you or anybody can do about it except let me count to twenty and then kiss me—no—not anybody—just you!—I'm madder than a Hatter — Damn! Damn! — — Don't let it bother, however. Tomorrow, I'll wake up and say— "Sid—you're a damn idiot—What do you care—You're taking yourself too seriously—nuts"—Then I'll eat breakfast and forget about it — I've been angry now for a full twenty four hours ——That's the longest spree I've ever had — I'm strictly a fifteen minute grudge bearer!

Now to the brighter side—you—and a letter from you—The 26th— Since little of any consequence occurs these letters of necessity are merely replies and comments upon yours—which is only correct—You're the traveler now—the adventurer—You're meeting new people, doing different things—seeing new sights—Now its my turn to ask you to share your moments of pleasure, or unhappiness (which better not be often 'cause if there's anything I like to beat it's a gal named 'Stelle when she insists on being unhappy) — There's only one way to do these things—Grab the letter—a little ambition and — March!!

Some job this babe Taylor's doing keeping you on "the straight and narrow path"—two merchant marines, four navy fliers — some assistance

– phooey—with her as your roommate I'd best pack up my effects and say "Goodbye sweet dreams"…

Agreed— "Tolerance" "am" a word for intolerants who like to lie to themselves!…

So—I'm a "pretty nice guy"!—You had to travel half way across the country to find that out—Well its about time my propaganda began to take effect — I can see where your resistance is slowly but inevitably being crushed — Never mind this flattery — just say "Sid—of course I'll marry you—the day after the war"—…If it takes the rest of my life I'm going to teach you to say yes –Yes??

Questions—questions— "We are lucky, you know it?"—(what kind declarative, interrogative sentence is dis??) Not lucky—exactly—it probably could be worked out by complicated comparison of possibilities — — Take a ton of corn seeds—Put one beautiful sweet seed in the bin— then add a black one—ugly, sour, unpleasant—mix well—Pick up two— Well—see what happened—Besides we weren't brought together by the stars—we were just magnetized!…

"Do you think you could have loved anyone else as you love me!" – Most assuredly no!! —— I'm certain I have never wanted to please anyone more than you — I have never worried about anyone but you — I never could like someone else as a sister, complain to like a mother, confide in like to a father, joke and play with like with a friend, talk to like to myself — No one else makes me get hot and cold chills — makes me feel happy — then angry — then uncertain—then happy all over again — I have never sought another's arms — missed their embrace, want[ed] their strength and confidence — like I do yours—What the devil—You know how we are – not exactly unique — just mortised and tenoned together — We just are—

And we're not a "special combination" — She goes into a Chinese restaurant with American food and has nothing to write about—She looks at the menu under salads and sees "Special Combination." So right away I'm "lettuce" holding on to my tomatoe who's playing with the cole slaw—and we're both dunked in mayonnaise — and in between us stands a deviled egg!—"special combination"—There's nothing combining about us—We're just two North poles spinning each other around—only we like it—And deep down inside we know one of us is South pole — — And I love you so badly the linings of my heart, liver, kidneys and brain are thinning.

And if you say yes—you're a fool—If you say no—well—you're wise — — but—well — — I never could have such devotion and affection to anyone else—

Skip the politics—come here—that's good—let me hold you—very close—blow into your ear—kiss your cheek—lock my head in the hollow of your shoulder—Stop me!! — I get so I feel those things — What a guy's imagination can do—

> I am
> Your
> Sid

At Northwestern

Explaining my influence on him, Sid wrote: "It's just that every time I'd think of going to pot there'd be a voice— "Stelle won't like it' or— 'What would 'Stelle think'—Most of the time I'm "saved"—I feel so good and comfortable and near to you."

141

July 19
Darling,

A propos of nothing I am enclosing a page of the Pacific Pony edition of "Time." I'm not sure whether or not you've ever seen it—so—ici!—Its really revolutionary. No advertisements, no fancy frills, every ounce of paper utilized. The entire magazine folds up and is enclosed in a business size envelope and sent 1st class mail—Three days ago I received a copy of the July 10 edition—only seven days after date of magazine—…

Why all this?—Oh—just a warm feeling of complacency—a satisfaction with you—a comforting sensation of being "looked after"—by a swell gal.—A knowledge that she knows what I need almost instinctively—Well—I just feel good and parlor-sofa-ish. Someday someone will ask you why you bother with me—don't come to me—I'm sure I don't know—Perhaps its not right for me to so selfishly hoard you but sweet—well—you're peculiar with me—seriously—I've never had a yearning to collect things—Never saved match-book covers, trinkets,—once dabbled in philately—was bored—I keep no diary to save unpleasant memories—the pleasant ones always remain…I just don't go in for saving things. But, in your case an entirely new problem confronts me—I want to hoard you, collect you, save you—I want to build up a handsome collection of you—then share my treasure with the world—Like a jeweler I will boast of your beauty, carats, fineness, sparkle and let people's mouth drool with envy—only this little facet is not for sale — Just a greedy miser will I be insofar as you're concerned—I'll also love you —

Yesterday I had my first pepsi-cola in over a year—It was, well—luxurious—Its effervescent carbonation caused the throat to burn, lachrymation, internal turbulence. For a short moment I was back in a little candy store at home drinking a pepsi-cola—smacking my lips after downing the last drop—tossing the nickel to the storekeep—For a moment this was a summers day after a handball game—or a Friday night late when I'd have a celery tonic at the delicatessen around the corner and the restauranteur would smile at the smudges of lipstick on my cheeks—Seems my skin had unique absorbing   powers—much better than Kleenex— — I liked it very much—no—dope—not the strawberry flavored lipstick!!! Why must you always twist my words around…? Wench!!…— it all boils down to—well I enjoyed every moment I spent with you—I want and hope to spend many more pleasant hours, days, weeks, months, years, decades, centuries with you —

Tonight I saw "In Our Time" with Ida Lupino in a nearby unit. — — It was okay — it moved slowly (too slowly) in the beginning. It had a purpose—a message capably and lucidly presented. The death of the old world the rise of the new in Poland. It was fairly bold and revealing—with the usual amount of flag waving for dear old Poland—Nothing to go out of one's way to see—Just a nice V for Victory affair which makes you want to believe you know what the hell you're fighting for...You know you have no mission to force democracy down the throats of the unwilling or those unprepared for it——You know damn well you'll not bless the natives with modern plumbing —... Maybe our "glorious" battle will bring a better world—but its so heart-breaking to sweat and strain for the shining words of freedom and read of prejudices at home, to listen to a New Zealander spout about "The white man's Burden—ya know—give 'em the bloody whip over the back"—To read of Poland's "free" army rejecting Jews,— — —

'Stelle I'm getting out of this war alive – with half a break — if I so much as open my mouth about politics — or people — or the world — kick me — hard — ...

Enough—it is late—tomorrow—after all—is another day ——

I love you—very much

Your

Sid

In responding to a "difficult" letter of mine, Sid tried to make me understand something of what he had been going through.

"There's the times when you roam the streets lonely and disgusted when you want to see how it feels to get stinking drunk — ——When the months away from home begin to gnaw at your mind — There's the times when the stink of the dead and the moan of the wounded make you feel awfully sorry for yourself—Values change, thoughts are shattered, dreams become hazes far off in the distance—so far—so very very far—The times when your mind says "quit"—The times when you'd laugh at a picture and all the while there's a hungry loneliness banging at your insides—How have you helped?—Just by being around, writing—saying nice things— joking—yes even scolding—you've been good to me and good for me—I don't know how to say this because—well—it doesn't need saying—you know how I feel about you."

Sid described what it felt like to be in a helpless position.

July 28

Darling,

...We were on an O.P. at hill X. It was atop a tall boulder. To get to the niche in the top one had to climb using some indentations cut into the rock for footholds. While going up or down one was completely exposed to the enemy. It was entered only after dark. One night the enemy attacked—We were but four atop the boulder Four men, four carbines, a box of grenades, a telephone and a radio that was all The enemy reached the top of the hill and began sniping –The pop-pop-pop-pop of the Nambus lights grated on your nerves—The toy pistol "pow" of the American carbines and the deep throated roar of the heavy machine gun—All—this of course means nothing except that on that rock there were four men who could do nothing—They daren't stick their heads up—They couldn't move—all they could do was wait and pray the line held—that the counter attack was successful—You just sat there—grasped your carbine firmly and felt weak—oh you could talk all right—you could make funny jokes and put on false bravado—You could discuss that babe in the Copacabana over the telephone to your rear C.P. but that couldn't make the people back there comprehend the situation—

Here I am 'Stelle—trying to make you understand how helpless I feel— ...can't you see—its having your hands tied—It's the feeling that whatever you do you'll get hurt—Its that aggravating sensation of just sitting and hoping—— that there's no sure way to turn—

'Stelle I love you and want you with every ounce of love and affection within me—

This all will undoubtedly sound like a very corny line which it is but— well—I think perhaps you've sometimes experienced the same emotions —

Your
Sid

July 29

Darling,

Last night an extremely humorous occurrence had us roaring all evening.

The gang was riding home in a jeep on the way home from a movie. Lt. Pflum was reminiscing about good old home —

"Boy would I like to have a good old fashioned hamburger"

Lt. MacClelland—"With mustard"

Lt. Pflum—"And a juicy slice of onion"

Capt. Van Yush—"All covered with catsup!"

Whereupon Lt. Pflum stopped the jeep, got out, threw his hat on the ground, and shouted

"The first God damned hamburger I've had in a year and you spoil it with catsup!!!"

You get that way after awhile—The usual stuff today—Look, you're working too hard—This diet of sandwiches and malted milks is either going to eliminate your end completely or leave me with a ghost to make love to—I love you—which is more than I can say for you—You take care of you—see!

Your
Sid

August 10
Darling,

Today we have eaten of my garden — Yes, the radishes have sprouted and we had some of them for luncheon. The delight of knowing that that which you eat is there as a direct result of your own labor is indescribable. No middle man for me, no money mad speculators, wholesalers, retailers, bankers,—Just a simple human digging the earth and reaping the benefits of his toil—…Do you think you could live on the earnings we make from our radish farm?—We could always eat the radishes we don't sell—The beans are budding—but I'm afraid the carrots are the black sheep of the family—they won't grow—

Yesterday I gave what I consider a successful lecture—The usual run of talks to strange outfits are dull, stereotyped—follow the outline affairs in an attempt to cram what took us two years to only half learn down the throats of unwilling infantrymen in six hours.

The one lecture was good because the subject matter could be stretched to only 15 minutes of a one hour period—So I just talked—the stuff went from feeble attempts at humor, to the history of chemical warfare to the weight of a mortar man's load on the march—You've done a lot of stage work—I guess you understand the exhilaration when you feel that the audience is with you—That they are sharing your story—Let us say that they were enthusiastic—

You get that reaction so infrequently that its immediately noticeable—

Which brings us to the three ringed circus of the 'Stelle-Sid extravaganza—Sometimes it gets a bit confusing—I'm just digging in and waiting—As soon as I can definitely determine the direction of your attack, the resources you have at hand,—I'll act— —Something tells me that if I'm pressed too much I'll withdraw—

I love you
Sid

145

Now the reason for Sid's saying that he might withdraw became clear.
He also discussed in this letter my discomfort with a clique of southern
girls in my dormitory at Northwestern. On political and social questions,
Sid and I were, and always had been, in perfect agreement. "Pinkish
nonsense" meant impersonal chitchat.

August 13
Darling,

I can endure this no longer—For a week now I've strived to stay sore
at you—No can do!——of all the classic faux pas you make 'em—"I love
you—but I can't forget Stan!" First I tried to laugh it off—Then well I got
nasty—then impersonal— leaving the conversation to pinkish nonsense.
Then—well—the old—sorry for myself gag!— So help me its just dawned
on me—You'll probably laugh or get angry—but I've discovered what
the hell love means!—Frankly my whole equilibrium was shaken—I was
jealous—with all the atavistic instincts within me I wanted to keep others
away from my mate—My God its astonishing—maybe it's the year or so
away but—I never felt this way before——Somehow it never occurred to
me –to be envious—I hate to act like a pig-headed jackass—but—for once
I want to own as well as be owned—I want to possess you completely—Its
not a swell relationship—intellectual companionship—occasional warmth
of a kiss—It's a maddening affection—a wanting, yearning—— for
you—Nothing else will satisfy—Perhaps I've "come of age"——You're
a part of me—The realization of how utterly and completely—What's
the use of being hypocritical—I just got to have you—When something
else threatens I feel like raving, roaring, biting, scratching like a mad lion
protecting his lair—

I love you—fervently!

The confession must be boring to my confessor literally—

Your "Studs Lonigan" incident is very funny—I read the book
when at high school—Farrel's not a very good writer—but he astounds
the ostriches who hide from the glaring facts before their eyes—Its
good to talk, act and participate in degeneracy but to have it exposed
to the limelight becomes vulgar and "Verboten"—Reminds me of our
chaplain…nice guy and all that—He's the reason why I read "Kings
Row"—I was told that after reading the first few pages he threw it
away in disgust—refused to put it back into the library—…So-oo——
We got hold of another copy and all read it—He's just that way—We
don't mind it—only serves as a good book reviewer for us—all those
he discards we read!—

As far as being radical—also brings to mind an incident—once in a discussion someone mentioned that C.C.N.Y. was a radical school.—I just blew my top—called them stupid, idiotic…I raised my voice—called them all Hearst underlings—Went on with a drool on propaganda——Once started I kept going until Lt. Pflum, the company commander very opportunely reminded me—"Lt. Diamond—you're raising your voice" Never had any trouble since—

Your troubles with the Negro question caused me to seek out a book I'd completed—"Selected Writings of Abraham Lincoln"—This comes from a letter to Joshua F. Speed—It was a harangue about the Nebraska, Kansas-free or slave state question. I think although written in 1855—it would be worthwhile considering now. "Our progress in degeneracy appears to me to be pretty rapid. As a nation we began by declaring that "all men are created equal." We now practically read it "All men are created equal except Negroes" When the Know Nothings get control, it will read "All men are created equal, except Negroes, foreigners, and Catholics." When it comes to this, I shall prefer emigrating to some country where they make no pretense of loving liberty—"…

Look—will you be happy? Darn it—Stop banging your head against a stone wall—You won't change them—And I'm certain they could never alter your views—Yours because they're right—theirs because its been ingrained within them from childhood——You make me fume because instead of enjoying your stay at Northwestern to the fullest you allow it to be soured by such incidents—…

So long sweet—Got to go to a special school for orientation officers—Why must they have 'em at night during our spare time—They tell me there'll be a movie afterwards—that's good—

Listen—bub—You're mine see And—I'm yours—see—'Tis not two individuals—'Tis one—Not "us" but a singular expression unknown to our vocabulary—a oneness—I'll prove it to you—if I have to marry you to do it——sweet, lovable—darling—You're okay—

Your
Sid
definitely—

Now all was well. The question of "Stan" was apparently dormant at the moment.

August 14, 1944
Darling—

First—I'm a heel—second—I feel like a heel—third—Don't t you tell me I'm not! Sometimes I wonder why you tolerate me—no cracks—you know you love me—I know damn well its reciprocated What a future— full of strife, disagreements; misunderstandings—Frankly it sounds interesting— anything with you in it sounds interesting – particularly the Sid Diamond family.

You'll probably not forgive me for the recent altercation—at least not because you love me – let me bribe you – huh?—Heck—think of all the nice things that can be purchased with a penny—I know you though—you'll scurry off to a bank and make a deposit chuckling gleefully at the thought of the 2% interest on a penny—and how at my very graveside you'll be able to pay the digger an extra 10 cents to throw heavy rocks... Frankly, I think we should have a let off of steam—I feel so warm now—so close to you—...

Ah—yes—yes——-excuse while I take a breath—more—you know you're beautiful—Got your picture right here—the big one—Why waste time talking. Kiss me again—okay—okay—don't—I'll kiss you—Be still—tonight I feel gooey—I want to bite your ear lobe, blow in your ear—kiss the nape of your neck—to hold you close—to draw you to me—hard—'Stelle —'Stelle—I miss you—If there's something in this religion—'Stelle forgive me for leaving you—for being a stupid idiot—— If I get out of this mess whole I'm going to make you the happiest woman in the world—I don't know how as yet but—somehow I feel ambitious for you—for us—We'll get there—

Wait and see.

You've been good to me—very good—Let me spend the rest of my life repaying you —War—hurry up and end—I craves my woman ——

I'm such a damn fool —- I'll not go off the deep end again—Only—you wait for me— see—and don't take my stubborn moments too seriously — You're supposed to kick me in the pants when I act that way—remember— Needn't bother this time— I've done it for you—endless times.

Yours—whether you want me or not—I belong to you—so there!

> I love you—
> Good night – sweet
> Sid

What a life——

The days are half endurable—but the nights—alone in my tent—with your picture—then there's the tossing and turning and trying to sleep— only you won't let me—you demand that I think of you—you come around and whisper in my ear—You stand outside in the moonlight and just look at me—You flirt with me—you scold— you smile—don't stop—come around every night—

I love you
Sid

August 15

Darling— sweet—

By the time this reaches you—the sixth anniversary of our meeting will have past —How long ago, yet so clear to the memory!—Self conscious because I needed a shave I stammered through our first meeting—Then it was just two kids playing handball—now its matured and blossomed into—a comradeship, devotion—the envy of all—Frankly—I've met a lot of people, talked for hours about love, marriage, etc.—haven't yet encountered a relationship that could equal ours—I like it—I like you— everything about you—The stray hair over the forehead, the nose—the ears—the neck—the body—the knees well—take it back on the knees— they hurt when you kick—The feet—the blisters you get so I have to make believe I'm helping you walk——I like your conversation—more for the times you don't make sense than when you do—I like the way you're well—cute—I like you when you're serious—Nothing about you displeases me—I like your firmness of opinion —Darn it all—You're a big business—but no liabilities—I love you—...

As orientation officer for my company I usually give an hour lecture a week—Lt. Brooks our Information and Education officer—gets another hour. During these talks we have to cover the war situation on all fronts and usually get some educational stuff in—Thursday, for instance, I'll talk about the Moscow Conference, its results as compared with the tripartite axis treaty—I'm also voting officer for the company—With all the different regulations prescribed for registration by the individual states it was quite a task to get the ball rolling—...I ended up by interviewing each man in the company—going over the requirements in his state and finally can say that at least 75% if not more of the men have applied for a state absentee ballot...

You've been getting extra long letters from me because—I like to write to you—so—objections overruled! You get long letters whether

149

you want 'em or not—And I'll tell you I love you as much as I want—
and we'll have no back talk from you except in kind —

> Your
> Sid

Once again in a light-hearted mood, Sid was able to see us as a two-person team.

17 August 1944
Subject: Miss Estelle Spero
To: the world

On several occasions there has been questions posed as to rank and authority in the Diamond combat team. Also some people have asked about who is most beautiful. – The following paragraphs supercede any previous bulletins on these matters.

Commander of the organization will be Miss Estelle, who upon assuming command will be responsible for the maintenance of discipline amongst her subordinates in particular Lt Diamond. Miss Estelle will be charged with the morale and well being of this officer. Lt. Diamond will assist in all possible ways and continue to show the same respect and affection to his superiors. Careful studies of photograph II MIAI – GARFIELD indicate that the C.O. is by far the best proportioned, most attractive of all models heretofore presented—The mark IAI reveals the following assets:

> irresistable lips
> clear vision –
> black, long eyelashes
> long flowing hair, slightly kinky
> eyebrows (note: one must be careful of these, when they are raised, duck for cover, when normal, proceed as usual, when lowered and wrinkles form at brow, kiss lips immediately —- or else hear the burst of a severe tongue lashing)
> Nose — very adaptable for biting —- also very pretty.
> Ears — Be careful of these. They are usually hidden and well camouflaged
> — If you get too close you will be caught by booby trap

M2 EARRING—they are excellent receptacles for hot air but
receive best when the truth is told—

the neck is streamlined and especially designed to overcome
wind resistance

the overall picture indicates an extremely efficient fighting
machine combined with an obvious beauty which is
dangerous for the unschooled—Although rugged in
appearance it has a few delicate mechanisms which must
not be fooled with by the novice–

the instrument on the whole has no liabilities that we can see

We recommend that this equipment be requisitioned for Lt. Diamond's
organization and that they get married at the earliest possible moment —
Despite Lt. Diamond's demonstrated lack of skill in handling this equipment
we feel he is sufficiently interested to study and learn this instrument —
its nomenclature, its functions, its use, its quirks and needs. He will be
responsible for the care of this instrument. This item is a critical one and
numerous requisitions have been made for it. Lt. Diamond, however, has
A-1 priority as soon as it becomes available.

General E. Motors

The picture Sid was looking at

The problem of "Stan" and Sid's threatened "withdrawal" took several letters back-and-forth over several weeks, to clear up. ("Fingers" was children's way of asking for cessation of hostilities.)

Aug.27

...It <u>is</u> a Sid-'Stelle "extravaganza"—a great show—The best show on earth—It glitters with radiant flashes and somber backgrounds—Its our production 'Stelle—a colossal affair of great magnitude and importance to both of us—The show is great because its got the best cast—its players, you and I—are superb because the parts were made for us and we were made for the parts. This show's in for a perpetual run— 'Stelle—darling— we just fit together—Heck my arms were measured so that they could fit around you—Couldn't possibly be used elsewise—And your lips fit mine—And your hair is the only hair I like to snuggle in—We were made a height suitable for giving each other "gentle" kicks without undue strain— We differ little in our opinions and interests—only I'm a pain in the neck because I'm stubborn—

As for the "military strategy"—Well—my fault again—Over here we call it poor "estimation of the situation"....

For a while, due to my own momentary break down of morale, uncertainty,—and "lack of understanding" (mine)—the situation looked grave—a "withdrawal" seemed imminent—Then I again weighed the issues—no sir—I wasn't going to quit—There was too much at stake. I needed you too badly—I loved you. Without you—life—well—wouldn't be worth much so I pulled a Japanese trick of attacking with "great dash and boldness"—I know this much, whatever happens I'm digging in—I'm not giving up easily—I'm keeping you and fighting for you to the bitter end—so there!!—And all the 40 suitors best beware—...

Sweetheart—look—I don't want you ever to feel that I doubt you—Heck—I trust you completely—because well—that's the way <u>we</u> are—both gentlemen—You more than me—I—well—that outburst was caused—well—perhaps a bit psycho—at the time—Brooding, nervous, uncertain,—These attacks occur about once every four months or so—just realize—I've been away over a year and well—I get awful homesick for you sometimes—And when it gets too bad I take it out on you...

I love you—Everything's okay— "fingers"

<u>Your</u>

Sid

August 28

Darling.—sweet—

Today's been another hot sultry day climaxed by rain. Oh well—lets not talk about the weather lets talk about—lets—say—us—We're okay now I hope I hope I hope!—I'm very much in need of you—Your letters mean very much to me—And I love you....

'Stelle, you've been very kind to me—more than you can realize—Not the material things like gifts and books—but well—you've kept a warmth and happiness glowing within me to which I shall be eternally grateful. In the drab and rotten existence of the tropics—the memory of you—fills the days and half the nights with pleasant thoughts—you—were, are, and always will be—one swell guy!—You and your happiness mean so much to me—...

The war news in the European theater sounds encouraging—Very encouraging—Maybe we can get this mess over with in another two years or so—less I hope—which recalls to mind Mrs. Roosevelt's classic crack that in the interest of public health men returning from the South Pacific should be kept in camps for six months for observation before being released—Sister—right there she became very unpopular—with me—

I don't doubt but that I've got malaria dormant in me and that upon the stopping of atabrine it'll break out but I'll be damned if I think there's any need for such nonsense as she proposes. Oh well—her noise has had no apparent effect so why should I worry—... Do you—will you——marry me?—I mean quick—before I get practical or you get fears—Our love probably was not forged in heaven but cast in the fiery furnaces of hades but there's no way of breaking the tie—Just welded together—very tightly—

Tonight—how about visiting my tent—We'll be all alone—say about 11:00 P.M.. There's not much room—but I'd gladly share it with you— There won't be any light—taps is at 10—but I won't have to see you—I'll feel your presence—I'll know you're there—It's a date—

Your—your very own
Sid

"Stan" was finally explained in my letter—of which, unfortunately, I have no copy. I do remember that my original reference was to a humorous incident which I thought Sid would remember. And Sid now was overjoyed to get the explanation!

August 29

Darling—my little "Femme Fatale"—

This is the second letter today—you keep still—If I want to talk I will!—I want to talk because well—I received your letter in which that "Stan" case was settled.— 'Stelle—I don't know if you're laughing as much as I am but you should—This is one time I'll let you laugh with me at me—whatta dope!—Chalk one for 'Stelle!—While in the horrible throes of "love's labor lost" I did think about Stan of A.P.O. but I still don't recall the incident you bring to mind—Please enlighten me further— I'll probably laugh all the harder—I was about to shoot poor innocent "Stan"—see all the bloodshed you would have caused!—Jezebel!!—The little affair had certain good results—At last we find out exactly how I would really react—I always thought I'd just "withdraw" unobtrusively if you sought another but now I know— —I want you very badly—need you even more than that——You crumb—you made me get out of my shell and rave and rant—opening closets to find skeletons, poking tridents under beds—okay—okay—laugh—Did you ever come to think of how poor Stan's mother would feel when she found his body bathed in blood— And the papers would read "He didn't have an enemy in the world."...I'm very happy—Thanks!—...

You're wonderful—And I'm not saying that to be nice—I wouldn't be nice to you—you "Salome"—cut my head off and dance with it on a tray—fiend—Have secret affairs with people named Stan who have "doity pichas" on the wall—with velvet no less!...o-o-o-oh—when I think of it—I could kick myself twice and you twenty times—and I will too—just wait and see——Darling, Darling, darling—I could literally smother you with kisses—Tomorrow when it rains—I'll strut through the damn thing singing—"You are my sunshine"—Sweet—if I weren't so lazy I'd jump in the air—click my heels—three times—What?—you don't think I could do it?—Neither do I—Be still—don't spoil my fun—If there were door bells around I'd go around ringing 'em—I'd stop people on the street and say— I'm a dope but she's marvelous!—— If I weren't an officer full of decorum and stuff I'd let out a howl of joy—— —yee-ee-ee-ow-ow-ow!!! I love you, I love you, I love you...I could hug you to death—Whatta relief!— I feel sufficiently intoxicated by this great happiness that I could dance the Conga with gestures—...I feel like grabbing your hand and running, anywhere, anyplace—just as long as you're with me—— Sweet—Sweet— Sweet—I want to grab you and whirl you around—around and around and around—Bombs, machine guns, artillery fire, I can take—but not a period such as the last two weeks or so—very bad for my digestion!—My sophisticate, my devil, my virago, termagant, witch, wench, beast, cur,

Satan with horns that spit fire, temptress of men (me particularly)—most beautiful of the beautiful, vamp, siren, I love you——I'd better stop lest I spoil you –

Your—oh so very much
Your Sid

Thanks again—

The reorganization of the battalion and Sid's assignment to a different company were disturbing.

Sept. 3
Darling—

I'm going to cry on your shoulder again, so get out the rubber sheet. We'll begin at the beginning which is always a good place to start. You recall I said that as a result of the reorganization in the battalion I might lose my executive officership. Well Sam—Sam Hindman—former exec was transferred back from Hqs. Company where he'd been ammunition and motor officer. So that put me back as platoon leader of the third platoon— This is the way my Company Commander broke the news—"I'd probably like to keep you as exec—Lt. Hindman's outranking you doesn't mean anything, only I want my strongest line officers leading the platoons"— So—big strong officer that I am I take over the platoon. Things weren't so bad—I knew the men, they knew me. We'd been together almost two years and we'd gotten to know each others good and bad points. Been through our first action together and all that sort of thing.

Well—yesterday—Sept. 2, 1944 it happened—I was transferred to Company "C"—It isn't a bad set up—only I don't know my men—I don't know what they can do, how well they can do it, and where their weaknesses lie—You don't get that knowledge overnight—Its by constant living together in close contact that such knowledge is attained—Its difficult to explain but a platoon leader has to have the utmost confidence in his men—He's got to—

I don't doubt but that the men under me now are as good, if not better, than my former platoon but one thing I've learned from long experience in the army—Never make any assumptions!—

The Company Commander, Lt. MacClelland—pretty good egg— Other platoon leaders—Lt. Buchner, Lt. Butler – (from Brooklyn)—the Company Exec is Lt. Bochstahler—from Indiana—a Phi Beta Kappa boy—And the platoon executive officers are Lt. Foster—If you recall he used to be my exec. a long time ago—Lt. Lonquist or something—He's a replacement that just joined us—My platoon as yet has no executive officer and—I've got a hunch I won't have one for a couple of weeks which also doesn't do me any good. I could go on for days but it won't help....

Last night I saw the motion picture "Battle of New Britain"—I believe it's been shown in the states under the name of "Attack" I'm not sure—One of these uncut things, factual—etc.—It is my honest opinion that every one at home should be forced to see this picture—Perhaps it would give them a little idea of what fighting in the South Pacific's like—We could talk and write from now till doomsday but it would take seeing—such as you do in this film to understand our difficulties—To comprehend why in Europe they go 50 miles a day and here 500 yds. in a day is excellent—

Darling, haven't received mail from you in a couple of days—I miss them very much my little "morale-builder-upper and downer" Its hot today—but not more than usual.—Have you moved to your new home yet? Whats it like? I've already moved down to "C" Company. My new <u>home</u> is almost the same as my old one only I haven't had enough time to slop it up as thoroughly as my previous quarters. 'Stelle—I love you—very much—— I feel like just sitting on the couch, holding your hand—not talking, just sitting—It's a date—I love you—again?—Still!

Your
Sid

Now I go to memorizing the names of the men in my platoon—God—you know the difficulties I have in remembering names and people—That's about the hardest blow of them all—

With the defeat of the Japanese on Bougainville in April, there was much-needed opportunity for recreation. A battalion site had been cleared, and USO shows came through. There were softball and basketball games and evening movies. At the same time, training for what lay ahead continued.

Sept. 4
Darling,
...Today—today I gave a lecture with a public address system!—First time I'd been in front of one of those damn microphones. Ye Gods—your racket's more hazardous than mine. I'm not fooling. When required I can usually "drill voice" a lecture for a short time but this was a two hour affair with a large audience—I've talked about the 4.2 mortar until I'm blue and black in the face but this took the cake. Ordinarily I like to pace back and forth slightly as I talk. This type of talk requires moving from blackboard, to chart, to demonstration, back to chart—and so on—Think of me—struggling

156

from one side of the platform to another dragging that damned mike all over the place. And it never would stay at the right height. You laugh at it in the movies but this darn thing would sink as I spoke and I'd gradually bend down lower and lower and lower—Then in desperation I'd raise it only to go too far and find myself stretching my neck like a swan after crumbs....Seriously—it exhausted me—mike fright or something. Well—Just 3 more like that and then I'm done—at last long last—done with those darn things!...

I was gone for awhile—now back again—Put me back on the front lines—this is too much—Routine training in the morning—A two hour spiel in the afternoon and then—this evening 2 1/2 hour session on military law and court martial procedure—Now at 9:30 my work day is almost complete except for the pleasant task of writing you. Very saccharin I know but—well—I do like writing to you—

True—it can't compare with being with you, embracing you—feeling the warmth of you—It can't replace the conversations—gestures—dances—fun—work—excitement we both shared...But I can imagine us—me talking to you—Thank God I can't get any back talk for several weeks and by that time I've forgotten what I said...

Sweetheart—I love you very much—exuberantly—effervescently—extensively—all over—I do

Your
Sid

We enjoyed comparing our ideas about what kind of wedding we should have. Thinking about other aspects of the future remained a source of anxiety.

October 2
Darling,

You will make no cracks about any of the errors herein made or made herein. I am using a typewriter of unknown vintage with numerous devices omitted and several conveniences such as margin stops, ... conveniently absent...All I can do is sit back and sieve your letter for topical material...

Now I can see what I'm up against in this marriage deal...It certainly is not the kind of fuss and noise I want—I assure you I will be very obnoxious to your relatives, my relatives, and the rabbi if he makes a long speech. I will flirt with all your female friends, leer at all the male friends and make a date with Pearl for the next evening—And I won't be found in those ridiculous tails—Get the ushers and your family to wear fancy duds I'm coming in shorts and sneakers—While we're talking lets face some facts unpleasant though they are.— Regardless of how much I want to do the thing up right for your sake—Maybe if I'm lucky—after another six months or so I get a twenty one day leave—21 days—to crowd two years of separation—then back to this mess—back to the same job. If anything its going to have to be a quickie—Then again you may change your mind—what the hell I've changed a little—Maybe you have—I don't know. Well I'll let you worry about that—I'm your property—whatever you want to do I do to. How about a small one right away and a big one when I come back to stay???? No ????I didn't think you'd approve...

Cousin Edith now on her last leg at college writes that she's doing student teaching at Erasmus High in Art, works two nights a week and has time to go around to hospitals and paint portraits for wounded soldiers— She sent a picture—Now I got two pin up girls.

Sunday—that was yesterday I felt particularly "nothing-to-doish" so I grabbed a jeep and drove around for awhile. It wasn't very satisfying— The roads were bad as a result of the constant rain. Accordion pleated is the only suitable description of that road.—Very bad for the "end"—

Also got a note from Ida—Works in State Lab as immunologist – went around the outlying sections—collected deposits for blood banks—200 pints!!!! – Some people's children—

Me?—fraught with wonderment about the future—Everybody's working at something constructive—and me with my "profession"—Oh well—I'll worry about getting back in one piece—Then I'll think about the future—Almost 2 1/2 years away from school—and I forget so easily—...

Right now—I'm very much in love with you—which is very easy to understand...

I am—Your—
Sid—always—

Sid described another kind of battle, without guns or mortars.

Oct. 8, 1944

...Well, we've been in another scrap—No, not against bullets, mortals, or mortals' machines but against nature, against jungle, against tropics——Last night a heavy wind blew in from the sea—It whistled and howled and raved through the island. Accompanying the violent winds was a torrential downpour—Trees swayed in large crazy arcs, their trunks bent before the wind.—Rotten old branches began to break from the mother tree and fall around the area— Such is the way of the jungle—Rot the insides and with one push crush!—So it was with the trees—The night was punctuated by the crashing of the trees. The occasional cry of "Look out!"—Most men sought shelter from the rain in their tents; some even slept!—Scant protection against falling timber!!!—— After a few unfortunate mishaps—we were all up—searching for a place where trees could not fall—we crowded into the mess hall— The wind growled. Mahoganies, rotten inside, screamed in anguish, and crashed to earth. A wiseacre whispered— "Jeez—they got our position bracketed!" Nobody laughed.— Flashlights, lanterns, candles burned throughout the area—Men dashed about with fearful eyes watching the skies!—Like in all battles—there were casualties—only a couple, fortunately and not too badly hurt.—— This morning, as if in a fit of rage against the jungle for its despicable attack the night before we began to cut trees—cut—cut—cut—Cut every damned tree that could possibly fall near us—Saw, axe, machete went wild in their enthusiasm.—Men sweated— gritted their teeth—but at each cry of "Timber!" there appeared a satisfied grin on their faces.—They worked like demons—Never had a field of fire for their guns been cleared this quickly—— Now the trees are gone—the trees we had left to shield us from the jungle's sun—to camouflage us from enemy observation. Now destroyed—to protect us from the jungle's might!—This phase of our fight against tropical hell seems successful—Let the monsoons blow—We've won this battle!—I wonder??

That—covers—that—Now you know what I did yesterday evening and today—...

I'll need no rehabilitation as far as you're concerned....—Hell—I like you because you're you—— You'll always be that way...I like her...I like her talk, her wit—her seriousness, her unnecessary worrying...

I miss you very much, darling—I want to be home with you...and say nothing—— but—I love you

> Your—
> Sid

To have his skill as a soldier recognized and praised was very satisfying.

Oct. 12
Darling—

...At present I feel pretty good.—Why?—Well—here's the story – A couple of days ago Mac (Lt. McClelland–Co. Cmdr.) approached me and asked, "How would you like to assault a fortified position?" Immediately I suspected a rat—Maybe they've found a few Japs somewhere and here I go traipsing a couple of miles through the jungle— "Not particularly" was my reply—

"Be ready to move out on a reconnaisance at 1000"—The crumb apparently likes to make people sweat—It was only after I made contact with the infantry that I discovered it was only a demonstration that'd last just one morning. What got me mad was that they had me on the spot.—— but literally—A couple of generals and brass hats around to watch plus most of the officers from the battalion. It was this latter group that annoyed me most.— If I didn't get in on the target I'd have to stand the ribbing from now till the end of the war.—— I usually work or play best when I'm mad—(witness the fact that I beat you once in seven games of ping pong when angry but never could do it at any other time)—So I fixed 'em. Registered on one target with only two rounds—got a rating of excellent—— So that's that—and I feel very self satisfied, complacent—Very enthused about the superb work put out by my gun crews—I think my new platoon will be okay—...

I'm staying up late to write this—Its after ten—after taps—all the lights are out but mine—The darkness crowds around my tent—come—come to me now sweet—We're alone—together...

> I love you
> Sincerely—deeply
> Your
> Sid

Oct. 23

Darling,

...What's new in Chicago? Your proposed schedule sounds full and interesting. Usherette, sophisticate, scholar, actress, directress, tutor,— ad infinitum—If people ask me what 'Stelle's doing I'm going to be in a helluva fix.

"Wee-e-ll—She's a member of the musicians union –er—She's working on a couple of prospective jobs in radio—er—eh—Going to school—What(?) – Day or night (?) – You got me there—— er—she writes continuity, visits instructors—writes to me and calls me naïve—Cooks meals of dubious quality (I need proof) —Reads books – Drives me crazy from love and exasperation. She also looks beautiful—is beautiful—Here—take a look at her picture—What?—How'd she ever fall for me?—We-ell—I've got certain charms.—What?—Where?—Now you've really stumped me!...

Enough!!—I love you, sweetheart—extensively—narrowly— overwhelmingly

> Your Sid

Oct. 24

…'Stelle,—you know—I've been thinking what will happen when and if I ever get home—Frankly, between you and me—I'm afraid of it—I've changed a lot—I don't talk as much as before—I find little to laugh at—I shun political discussions—— I'm growing very introverted—— Oh well—…

And I never got angry with you—just Stan!!—I couldn't be angry with you—

'Stelle— 'Stelle— 'Stelle— 'Stelle— I love you oh so very much—— You're going to need a lot of patience and understanding—— I'm going to need a lot of improvement————————

The dashes and long silences are just there—Just a lot of things that can't be said—A lot of childish fears, a lot of confusions, a lot of uncertainty—— Strange—How a guy with my "profession" worries so little about getting hurt physically— 'Stelle—don't let me ever stop dreaming—It's the future that anchors this whirling nonentity—— …

Darling—To have you tonight—To hold you—envelop you with my arms… To here you say again— "I love you" —…Let's never grow too old to hold hands in public—I love you

Your

Sid

About this time the battalion was alerted for movement.

4.2 mortars set out for inspection   Sid with theodolite, or transit

In Sid's letter of November 1, the weariness and sadness evident in his ruminations made me yearn to comfort him. He seemed to be looking over the "terrain" of his months of service from a high vantage point which provided a more encompassing and discouraging view than he had described previously.

Nov. 1, 1944

Darling,

Almost seventeen months overseas. It seems like such an endless interlude. Yet, somehow, the day of departure is so clear.— The way we walked from camp through sidestreets to the pier. There were no bands, no flourishes, few people. A few lonely citizens watched us go by with a dull expression of having seen the show before. Many other troops, on many other days had preceded us—and there were many more days and troops to come. A woman cried. A young girl waved. The men were too hot and impressed by the occasion to whistle at her. Then the morning when the ship went around the harbor checking the instruments. We did a lot of thinking that morning.

There was a peculiar sensation that all this wasn't new – that our ancestors somewhere had experienced the same tightening around the stomach. Perhaps the feeling was inherited from our animal forebears. Were we not about to engage in the birthright of beasts?—soon we were to live, eat, hate, fight like the beasts of yesteryear. Man hadn't changed much. Sure, we had tanks, carbines, mortars, planes—They were only aids to man's atavism.

Some of us felt cheated—We had gambled but believed our losses to be excessive. The man with the new born baby, the man who just got married, the younger boys who wanted only to live in dreams of youth— no, 'Stelle—There were no bands!

Then in retrospect came the second departure —— A soldier always "departs" he never "arrives"—When we left New Caledonia—We'd gone speeding through the streets of the capital city —

More departures, more thoughts, more wondering about the "arrival"— Each island is only a place to depart from to go to another island —You never get where you're going. The morale services and motion picture heroes say we won't stop until we reach Tokyo – We know our departures, leave takings, will never end—Sometimes one wonders as he sees the white crosses neatly lined up in well formed ranks—Sometimes the cemetery brings the question to one's mind —— Are these the men who have finally "arrived"? The chaplain calls them the "departed" ones—but their journey is over — "Last Stop—All Out!"

This letter may well be titled "Random melancholias" and politely dumped into a trash basket.

The ghost of Johnny Martin parades before us now—a nice kid—about twenty—The army hadn't aged him much—He laughed a lot. Johnny never complained. I can remember, so vividly, so cruelly clear—our last few days before we left the states. We had a beer party. Johnny played the guitar and sang western and hill billy music – Sometimes, when I'm not watching myself I catch myself humming the "Truck Drivers Blues" his favorite—They didn't allow men to carry excess baggage so I carried his guitar with my equipment when we left.—Martin wasn't brilliant. What he lacked in education he made up for by his cheerfulness and eternal smile—He was just another guy—who got off at the "end of the line."

Don't mind this morbid nonsense. Sometimes the loneliness overwhelms me— the noises of the insects, birds, small creatures seem to crowd into my tent crushing against me. It is terrible to live with memories only.—The soldier doesn't think of the future. His "present" just exists and the Past is all he can think about

'Stelle I wouldn't write or speak this load to anyone but you because it sounds so childish and you're the only one to whom I can moan. Reminds me of a ditty make up fad we have here. Once I complained about some nonsense so now, every time I open my mouth I'm greeted with a

"Moan and groan
With Sidney Diamon"
Ted Bochstahler gets
"Yell and holler
With Ted Bochstahler"
And so on —

Anyway I'm moaning and groaning on your very nice, soft shoulders— I want to be with you—I love you.

Your
Sid

The very next day the 82ⁿᵈ Chemical Battalion was on the move again. Sid's spirit and belief in what he was doing were revived by what he saw.

Nov. 2 '44
Darling,

Again,—a short note—We've been moving so fast, so often, so far – that we just can't squeeze in mail —I'm writing this in the courtyard of some large Filipino commercial house—they say we'll stop for two hours – so – a letter to you—a little rest for me —

There are so many things to say—so many new sights, customs, terrain, emotions that this little postcard can scarce do justice —There is one point though that I'd like to bring out – Perhaps you'll understand—Sometimes while slapping away in the jungles there arises the great big "What the hell am I in this for?"—well, I know now—Regulations prohibit atrocity stories in the mail but for unmitigated brutality— barbarism— cruelty—the Japanese take the grand prize.

Emotions are difficult to transcribe on paper but I'm glad I'm here – I'm glad we've helped these people and hope we can drive the enemy out of the Philippines quickly.

My thoughts are with you constantly—sometimes I welcome night— so that I can stretch out on my back— feel around for a comfortable position in my hole—then look at the stars and think of home and you—also cuss my feet for burning—We walk and walk —

No trouble so far—I think I'll be okay —

> I love you –
> Your —
> Sid

Rest and renewed spirit brought a revival of humor. I was at Northwestern, changing addresses and causing Sid some doubts about where to address his letters and the flowers he sent every month or two, when it was at all possible. (This letter was typed, and Sid used "dots" instead of dashes.)

Nov. 3

Sweetheart,

Occasionally I am seized by pangs of guilt ….The aforementioned sensation stems from reading some of my own handwriting ….I have always suspected that you didn't actually read my letters … just scanned through them, as you would a paper written in Tonkinese ….. and remarked "I wish I had time to study that strange language … It must be fascinating."…You must grow weary of those outlandish sheets of Micronesian hieroglyphics that the mailman deposits at your doorstep so irregularly. I'll admit they undoubtedly intrigue you because of their anthropological import …. With your customary scholarly attitude you fondle the parchments and drool in scientific ecstasy….. "At long last …. The missing link … I have discovered remains of the transitional period between primates and homo sapiens … here are evidences that this intermediary civilization had a primitive means of communication …. But I wonder what the hell it says!!!"…. With this in mind I have taken a slug of Schlenley's Reserve and attacked this decrepit machine … I'll agree that the attempt at typing will not show any marked improvement over the written stuff …. You can't shoot me for trying … Knowing you I make that last statement "tongue in cheek" as the saying goes …

Today has been a banner affair … A New Yorker and a package from you .. The package contained three books, stationary, stamps, candy and of course a fruitcake …. Deny me my books .. deprive me of stamps .. Steal

165

my candy ... but never .. never forget my fruitcake ... fruitcake ... the very word brings visions of luxurious mansions with tremendous courtyards .. A harem of beautiful fruitcakes dance before the hungry eyes of the Prince ... Little walnuts scurry amongst the pirouetting raisins and luscious red cherries intermingle with the rum drenched bandit fruits ... and it tastes good too .. The books .. "Father and Son"... "Crazy Like a Fox" ... "The Garden Party." I'll reserve comment until I have read them ...

A few nights ago we saw the motion picture "Till We Meet Again"... Being overseas for so long we are not usually hard to please but this last bit of unadulterated drivel is a travesty on any sane man's intelligence and when I include myself it must really be bad... You probably know the story .. A pretty novitiate at a French convent leaves the protected life of those preparing to become nuns to assist a downed American flier ... He's married and she's a semi-holy something or other ... Fifteen minutes after the plot developed everybody in the audience knew that she had to die .... And the author very obligingly got himself out of the pickle of having a spiritual love of a married man and woman pledged to God by having her killed in the end ... Frankly I prefer Hopalong Cassidy Gets his Man—at least you know it stinks before you get there and are prepared ....

More good news ... I don't deserve it I know but I've received a letter from you ... pardon me while I strut in self satisfied and disgustingly happy elation ... You're wonderful, marvelous, stupendous, sweet, pretty, sugary, spicey and glorious to love and I don't think there's another such creature in all of Gods heaven, man's Earth, or Satan's hell ... Kiss me darling before I collapse from sheer love of you ....

Let's take a look at this one ....You are having your troubles ..... Please don't move until the flowers get to you ... and when you do move let me know where to write ... I think Jan must be in love or something... an undesirable situation should be remedied ... I want you to be happy .... Do you think it wise to live alone .... There's nothing prudish or stuffy about that last crack... Being alone can be hell particularly when you're lonely ... Well you know best and you'll probably enjoy it more than you or I think ... I have my own tent and I assure you nothing could make me give up my privacy ... Personally I like living alone. The only companionship I need and need badly is yours ... We're a fallacy ... Two ones who when added together make one .. lets be alone together ... I could literally give myself to you ... as if I already haven't...

That graduate exam you're about to take sounds terrific... I could mumble some inanity about how "I'm sure you can do it" and let it go at that but why should I be kind to you? Are you kind to me? Hell no! You're a beast, a wench, Mephistopheles' sister, and I can't live without you...

166

Come into my kennel darling ... GR.—rr—rr woof.......I've got my fingers crossed ... why, I don't know, you'll be okay .....

And I know you're a hopeless neurotic and I know you're worthless and all the other nasty things you say about yourself but you just be careful how you talk about my 'Stelle .... See!! 'Stelle's not like that ... She has only one fault... She lies to herself... and sometimes believes it... she tells her stories to me 'cause I'm not afraid to tell her she's a fibber ... She's very nice, only don't tell her I said so,!!!! We are enemies-in-love until death...

My little frequenter of low dives ... What am I engaged to??? A fallen woman.. "Nana Spero" ... breaker of hearts ... torturer of men... addict of cokes ... I love you... Like the volcano on the island I rumble and growl ... My insides are a turmoil of bubbling, steaming, smoking affection —— Like the smoking monster I groan and complain because that which is in me cannot be unleashed .,.. Someday I will erupt and shower you with all the pent up frustrated amorphous mass of love within me... my weakened arms will grow strong from holding you .. Nothing will make me let go ... melted together in a flood of hot flowing lava... then crystallized into one rock that defies destruction. Think of me hard tonight... Save some room when you go to sleep ... I'm paying you a visit tonight ... I'll be beside you ... pressing you against me... rubbing my cheek against yours ... breathing into your ear... warming the chill of my nocturnal voyage with the heat of you ... Damn it all 'Stelle I need you and need you badly ... Stay with me and so help me I'll do my damnedest to get out of this mess in one whole piece...

> I love you—
> Sid

Nov. 13

Darling,

'Stelle, whenever I want to thank you for something I get marbles in my mouth. My customary loquaciousness leaves me. I always feel so damn humble and grateful.—What I'm trying to say is that I've read "Winesburg Ohio" "Crazy Like a Fox" and "A Walk in the Sun"—Darling I enjoyed them immensely...You just keep on picking my books—You're doing a "superior" job and <u>that's</u> putting it mildly. I'd like to hug you in gratitude and blow into your ear.

My letters have undoubtedly grown dull and slipshod but this inactivity, this waiting is getting us all on edge. I usually can pass most things off with a shrug but I can feel my nerves jangling occasionally. I need a kick in the pants from you. The kind you administer when you are really angry.— Ouch!!—Do you always have to take me literally??? Sunday Jack and I went swimming—We got to talking about Home. Jack's from Brooklyn.

167

He attended St. Johns University (or College?) in Brooklyn.—Didn't complete his course. We discussed the future.—I said that [if] I left the army before I was twenty five I'd finish school—Jack said that despite the so-called "G.I. Bill of Rights" he didn't see it—To put it in his words. —

"So you spend a couple of years at school—Then what?—the same uncertainty, the same insecurity—Why not spend the time working—" After some pros ands cons we both decided that if we both came out alive and whole we'd be getting off cheaply—and that that was the problem facing us.

"Step Right Up Folks! Come Closer! Don't block the traffic!! —That's right Mister – make Room for the Rest of 'em—Hurra, Hurrra, Hurra—Today we have something new, something daring.—Its sen-sational—Post War Plans – Hot off the griddle—Get 'em while they're sizzling—Get 'em now—There are only a few left on the market and we are practically giving them away!! And—And— Ladies and Gentlemen with each and every Post War Plan we are giving away—absolutely free—A new and ingenious discovery—Invented by one of our most famous and distinguished... dentists—Yes—siree—Here it is folks—The latest thing in "Readjustment"— A chromium plated, gilt edged, stainless steel "adjustment"—Guaranteed to last a life time—It will peel oranges, core apples, sharpen razor blades—It will make rubber stretch, it will grow hair on bald heads...! No home can afford to be without one—Get a Post War Plan now!!...

Sweetheart—I love you—Do you blame me?—You're swell—

Your—Sid

Nov. 16
Darling,

...There are some native boys around. The men are giving them some tobacco and peanuts—Funny how we call all natives "Joe."—You see 'em on the road and shout—"Hello Joe!" And they smile and yell back "Hello Joe"—

Speaking of languages and understanding them. The English speaking peoples of the world don't speak the same language. The New Zealanders are bad but I've yet to be able to make head or tails from the Australian gibberish—

"Hoi say—Got the toim??"

He repeated that about six times—my first reply was—"That outfits about a half mile to the left." After he pointed to his watch several times I got the idea!...

Sweetheart—I want you—Without you—all that exists is emptiness—Darling—you are good for me too—It is impossible for you to conceive how invaluable your constant, sustained and ever comforting love has been to me—Whatever happens to me, whether it be now or a hundred years from now know that with all my heart, mind, soul I am humbly and deeply grateful for your kindness and friendship—Your love and comradeship has made what might have been an ordinary and shabby growing up a mighty interlude of fun, laughter, talk, love, comfort—A warm healthy glow of life which flamed between us—You've made me very happy—I pray to be able to reciprocate—If I achieve half the happiness for you as you have for me—I will be satisfied—

> I love you, sweet
> Your
> Sid

Sid's thoughts were with me even as preparations were being made for battle.

Nov. 18, 1944
Darling
 – I've already written a letter today but well – I feel like being with you tonight —- I'd like to mess your hair up now —tease you—tell you your nose shows definite indications of a bibulous past—criticize your hat— just play—for awhile—then maybe we could just cuddle in each other's arms. And call each other nasty names like louse and stinker(?) – then you could drag out a book and read to us—I won't listen to the words—just your voice—and you could yell at me for not paying attention—sweet, sweet, sweet 'Stelle – I love you.
  'Stelle—look—well—wait—first promise you won't get angry— okay?—okay—About your living alone—Please don't—have somebody around you can talk to—I'm asking this as a favor—for a couple of more months—whatta ya say?? I just can't stand the thought of your ever being lonely—and alone—…I just realized it—I've been an officer two whole long years—About this time two years ago I was home with you—I pray, hope, beg that I be granted the opportunity to be with you next year—And for a long time thereafter—a very long time…
  I love you—yes <u>you</u> —

> Your
> Sid

Nov. 21

Darling,

Today I received your letter of Oct. 10th—..Something must have happened to the stamp...Took more than a month to get here.

You'd just seen "Voice of the Turtle"—And you couldn't get a record made of your voice and you put the check in the bank. Look—Ruler of my heart—Defender of My Faith—Lord over my soul— and pain in my neck—You drag out some of that money and spend it!—This instant!!!!—Okay, don't buy an evening gown but get something nice and enjoy it——Preferably not a handsome young man—

Speaking of that filthy stuff called money calls to mind a conversation which took place this afternoon:

He: —Boy, I've got my wife trained so she gives me detailed reports —

Me:—Why the hell don't you give 'er a check and forget about it.

He: —Do you send your money to 'Stelle

Me: —Some

He: —What does she do with it—

Me: — Puts it in the bank, I guess

He: —Does she send a statement from the bank

Me: —Hell—its hers as well as mine—Whatever she does is okay with me—

It ended about there—He doesn't realize that my big worry is trying to get you to use the stuff for yourself—I feel like going out with you tonight—Why don't you go out—make believe its with me—Tell me about it—— Go for a bus ride, maybe a show—drink several malteds—come home and then you and I can be alone—...

I've completed "The Garden Party" and "Fathers and Sons"—Turgenev was satisfactory—The pleasure of reading it was marred a bit by what appeared to be deliberate padding of the story with unnecessary descriptive matter—and irrelevant incidents—— It was Good—That is my personal opinion and cannot be considered as anywhere near an intelligent criticism.

Mansfield's "The Garden Party" set me back a bit. It was unusual—I'd never encountered a similar style—Sometimes I felt as if I were reading a young girl's book of the "Bobbsy Twins" variety, then I'd be astounded by a feeling of reading something profound—I can't share your complete enthusiasm for her stuff but I enjoyed it —

More books please—

Oh the letter also had a picture of you—Damn it all 'Stelle—You're wonderful—Sometimes people [gabble] that "Love" is blind but so help me you're tops—Way back in about June 1924 the people responsible for the construction of the earth's creatures must have had a serious confab:

Make Em Kwik: —What's the difference. Put in some salt, vinegar, malt, scotch, and call it Balyaso Spero.

Not so Fast: W-e-ell—Lets make something good this time.

Indy Ferrent: Ah nuts—whats the arg'ment 'bout—Get de usual—a little sweets, a lot of sours—a jig of love, a quart of temper, two fingers of stupidity, a gallon of ugliness and call it Hikela Spero

Not so Fast:—Its my turn now, you've been making all the rest— I'm making this one. — Here we go—two gallons of beauty, a quart of personality, a quart of brains. A gallon of intelligence, a gallon of friendliness, a pint of stubbornness, a thimblefull of hate, a fifth of temper, two gallons of comradeship—Mix 'em up well—Shake with an up and down motion— boil to living temperature—Then freeze quickly—Stamp Estelle Spero and deliver to Stork number 12 to be transshipped to the Spero household —

Joking aside—you keep getting nicer all the time—

I love you—very, very very much

> Your
> Sid

Nov. 30

Darling,

We've been busy as all hell…If this gets incoherent or I just fall off to sleep, please comprehend—Ah's jes weera!!—Bochstahler left for awhile. He was evacuated to another island for hospitalization—Jungle rot got him,—Nearly every one of us get a skin infection or fungus infection at some time or another and it can usually be controlled. Ted's just formed a large ulcer and it would take time and care to heal .

My own "itch" lies in the toes and some on thighs—It comes and goes—If I get wet and stay wet for a day out comes my annoying Krud, jungle itch, trench foot, or what have you—Its uncanny how it responds to certain stimuli namely wet damp clothing.

I don't particularly like this new island. Whereas before we complained of the interminable rain—Here its always hot and dry—The roads are a mass of dust. It is almost impossible to see as a result of the sand and dust. Sometimes, when the sand gets in your eyes, nose, mouth it resembles Don Anna in New Mexico where we went for rifle training and problems….

Sweetheart—my eyes are about to roll into their sockets…I'm s-o-o-o-o tired—I need you so much sweet

> Your
> Sid

On December 19, Sid mentioned not having received mail in several weeks. He enjoined me to take care of myself "and have all the joy and pleasures you desire of life—Miss nothing."

Dec. 24
Darling,

The God's are definitely good to this pariah, this sinner—this no-good loafer!! Mail!! Almost three weeks without a letter is a long time—I've already read your letters twice in the space of an hour. Gotta answer them right away—...

There also was a letter from Len—I quote—

"Life is wonderful of late——I have a room in town and am still there enjoying myself to the fullest extent of the articles of war —— I almost feel like a civilian—I'm going to concerts like a fiend—blah-blah——" Damn it all 'Stelle—I want to go home, to your arms—to you—I'm desperately lonely for you—I need you... 'Stelle—I don't understand it—I thought I did in the beginning but after what I've seen I can't comprehend why people fight—why there are wars—Why bodies, minds, souls are twisted, warped, torn—I think man is essentially animal—but God—what a beast!!!—I haven't seen any combat in a long time but all of its still vivid in my mind—Sometimes I talk to people about it—— Skip it—I'll cry on your shoulder for about an hour and then forget the whole deal —

The mail to you will probably be very irregular—I beg you not to worry —There is nothing wrong—I'll explain it all when I can—...

I love you darling—sweet.

Your

Sid

Now the 82nd Chemical Battalion was moving once again, to a new battleground, on navy transports, which afforded a taste of comparative luxury. As during previous voyages, Sid wrote often, gathering the pages into a very long letter. Excerpts follow.

Darling,

This is the third letter I've written—I hope I can complete this one without getting disgusted and tossing it away as I have the other two—we are aboard ship. The company is split up amongst the infantry units.—My platoon is with me—This is a large transport.—The biggest we've ever been on. Its clean—the food's good—(as on all navy ships)—There are no separate staterooms for officers as on L.S.T.'s—We sleep in bunks—arranged in tiers of three—there are about fifty officers in a compartment—We have a separate troop officers mess—until now there's been fresh eggs served for breakfast … every day!!!!-

As I sit here drinking bitter navy coffee the events of the past few weeks pass in an endless panorama. First the confusion and rush of getting set to leave —

Saying so-long to Butler, Katz, Mack, Foster and Lundquist—All of us are split up—on different ships with different units—The toast we drank that night — "May your dog tags never be separated!" The kiss that Jean gave to Butler, Katz and myself as if we'd known her all our lives—instead of being just three lonely lieutenants who listened to her talk about Dave, Dave, Dave— who'd left earlier. I talked about you. George asked her if she liked to have Dave call her beautiful. She didn't answer. I blurted that it wasn't necessary. If a girl's loved—knows she's loved—she can be certain that her beau thinks her the best —The conversation drooled around. Nothing worthwhile

Then the day of departure. How I worried about getting transportation to take us down to the beach. The heavy sea that turned the landing craft up on shore. The muddy beach road. The long, bouncing, wet trip to the ship. Then the going aboard. I've climbed up and down the side of navy ships in many types of weather but this was the worst —— Men would get halfway up the ladder and hang on for dear life as the ladder twisted back and forth—Some would get a little way up the ladder when a heavy swell would send the boat crashing into the man ——. I got a dose of it myself when I got on the ladder. I tried to rush up before the next swell but too late—the side of the boat caught me in the shins—result—bruised shins—Whatta way to fight a war!

Fortunately, outside of bruised legs, torn pants, and a good scare, nobody was injured—

So far the trip has been excellent. The transport is large enough to resist the ordinary violence of the sea—. So that I have not been ill once—For a man who invariably suffers from "mal de mer" that is a godsend.—…

The ship provides laundry service for all —And fresh water showers— —It is difficult for some people to realize what a trip in a navy vessel means. Its fresh food, cold drinks, hot showers, table cloths, glasses, real silverware—Its clean quarters without mud—Its relaxation—Its leisure— White glistening sinks and regular toilets that you flush—It is civilization —— It means hot buttered toast and chairs with backs to them—Oh well— we'll raise our girl to be a Wave or a Spar or something —— Don't you dare beget a son—One fool in the family is enough!!! And men are such idiots— all of us pitted against each other to battle until the end—What nonsense!

173

Perhaps it is our predestined fate that we shall destroy each other—Who knows?…Oh well—I'm too melancholy today to make sense—I'll continue this some other time…

'Stelle—its so peculiar—My unit is one of the few that have been in combat aboard ship. These poor jokers are so anxious to get their first taste.—You try and tell them what its like only they don't understand—I know they'll learn soon enough but—God —— lets skip it —— We could talk about the weather only that's usual—We could talk about you—only you already know how much I think of you and love you—And besides—should I spoil you with love?—hah?—

This is another day. Time passes slowly aboard ship. There is no mail to break the monotony of the voyage. Just the sea as constant companion. Being in the "nautical" frame of mind I read a couple of O'Neill's plays—"Anna Christie" "Hairy Ape" –It was the first time I'd read "Anna Christie"—No comment…Also read "Madame Bovary"—Flaubert.—These French authors are all the same—at least those whose books I've read—Zola, Voltaire, Gautier, Flaubert—Montaigne ——There is never a wife that's faithful to her husband. Never an old man who doesn't get on his knees to the fair goddess and beg for love.—Oh well—…

We continue this a few days later—Christmas is here—We are still aboard ship. We are anchored in a harbor for awhile…This afternoon I'm going ashore—I'll meet Jack and Mack in there I'm sure—Rubin and Cotton and Pflum were in yesterday—We had a sort of reunion—It was good to talk for awhile—I've made friends with most of the officers of the Infantry unit to which we are attached —…

I think I'll pack this letter away in an envelope and save it—I'll get it off as soon as I can—

"These are the times that try men's souls"…

Hope your visit to home proves pleasant and restful—Imagine your mom'll be glad to see you.

Apropos of everything—I'm in love with you

Your

Sid

I went home in mid-December for the Christmas holidays. It was wonderful to embrace and be embraced by my parents, to visit the Diamonds, to have some good times with old friends. But the thought of Sid and concern for his welfare never left me.

174

Sid's transport, on the way to the Philippines, stopped for some days at Manus Island, in the Admiralties, where this letter was written on Christmas Day. Sid's exhaustion—physical and psychological—is almost palpable.

Dec. 25, 1944
Darling,

Christmas occasions thoughts of warmth, of friendship, of giving—It says in all the papers!!—The spirit of the holiday, whether it be Chanukah, Christmas, or what have you is a noble and satisfying one. You and I agree that to give and love but once a year is close to the ridiculous—We, at least know the happiness of Christmas all year 'round. The pleasure of giving is ever present with us. It is not so much with the material creations that we reward each other but each day we give a little of ourselves to each other.—

It would sound inane for me to speak of how "different" our love is—— Somehow ours fills all the requirements. Poems, songs, stories of love and eternal devotion were written about everlasting, enduring, powerful affections such as the one which holds us together —

Don't mind the overdose of sentimentalism—Maybe it's the night—the radio which moans "Little Town of Bethlehem"—Perhaps the carols the men sang—or the quiet tropical night with the cool breeze and twinkling stars— or the remoteness of home— the loneliness of the moment—Yes today we had a community of thought. All the men—together—in a community of homesickness —— do not think harshly—or scoff at our childishness—We have so little—so little else but dreams —

It is difficult at present to be the cold, the practical.—Even more is it hard to be humorous or laugh— to joke—I cannot say where we are, what we are doing, what we will do—there's been so much between us unsaid and undone—So much of our lives missed —

'Stelle, for my part in this denial—I beg forgiveness—For my part in being such a fool, such a child —Will you understand? Sweetheart— Would I were with you so that I could tell you of these things. That I have contributed to your unhappiness—again—I humbly request you try and be patient with me—I would like to fill the air with plans, dreams, hopes —— But 'Stelle —— all there is, is a choking in the chest—Every once in awhile a guy gets himself overcome by despair; despondency overwhelms him.—it is so-oo long—so very very long —

I love you darling. —whatever happens—be happy—that's my only request—get everything we would have liked—fill your life ——(er—only keep my little niche open—so if I ever get home—I'll know there's one place waiting for me—— my corner of the world—Let it be a small alcove in your heart—put a comfortable chair there and always keep a warm fire glowing—Because if I come home in any recognizable form I'll head directly for that chair —That's where I belong—that's my home— with you—)

'Stelle, it's not weakness, it's not softness—it's a fact—I need you!!—I need you!! I need you!!—

Enough of this—I love you —"extensively"

Your
Sid

PART 4: 1945

With the start of a new year and good news coming from the Western front, the newspapers were promising huge New Year's celebrations in New York. Restaurants, night clubs, and hotels were sold out. Sid's transport continued its voyage toward the Philippines. (The letter from which this excerpt is taken was probably also written during the stopover on Manus Island.)

Jan. 1, 1945
Darling,
    ...Today is New Years day here—About now you'll probably be celebrating New Years Eve—— We heard in the daily news report that New York was planning the biggest New Year's celebration it had ever had—We were all very angry —— Maybe its because we're on a ship going to another hell as far as we are concerned—Maybe it's because the only way we knew it was New Year's was by the date on the order of the day – I don't know—it's hard to explain—Anyway to you, my darling, my sincerest —— my wholehearted wish that all you desire will be yours in the coming year....
    One of the unpleasant features of these little trips is lack of mail—I wish I could know psychically how you are—what you're doing. —
    Its unnecessary for me to describe my extreme devotion to you—I'm sure you must know it—feel it—Sweetheart—I love you overwhelmingly—I love you, I love you, 'Stelle dearest—I love you

Your
Sid

I attempted to explain, as best I could, the reasons for the celebrations which so angered Sid and his men, and to assure him that my thoughts and love were with him.

Sweetheart,
    ...Dearest, the emptiness of everything without you is appalling. The simplest things depend on you ... a walk, a conversation, a whim ... everything needs you for completion and enjoyment. Those people who made New York's New Year's Eve the biggest ever—don't be angry with them. They are seeking the distraction of drink and loud noise. There's no fun for anyone, any more, not in horns or night clubs. Don't condemn them. The crowds are engaged in mass escape. You can't blame them for trying. The spending, the shouting are not signs of happiness, you know that. The greatest happiness is still at a hearth, home, and now homes are

no more. You can't blame people for trying their damnedest to escape into something new for a while.

I love you, Sid. Don't forget. You're my guy, I belong to you.

Estelle

On January 9, infantry divisions and 4.2 chemical mortar companies accompanying or leading them arrived at Lingayen Gulf, Luzon, to begin the ground phase of the war to take back the Philippines. Sid still managed to dash off the following note.

Jan. 19, 1945
Darling,
Somewhere in the Philippines—In combat again—a lot to say but—A. very tired —B. very very dirty.—C. Busy, Busy as all hell—Been moving constantly—Excuse brevity—I love you—you make my fox hole warm and soft —— Sweetheart —

Your
Sid

I had to hope that the lack of mail after February was due to Sid's being too busy in battle to write or that mail service had been disrupted or that he was once again on the move to another destination. I was continuing my studies at Northwestern University. "SAD," mentioned at the end of the letter, was my sobriquet for Sid: "Such a Darling."
(This letter was a V-mail.)

Evanston, Illinois
March 1, 1945
Darling,
I'm listening to President Roosevelt as I write. I have been concentrating on him, but it wasn't worth it. He has said, fifty different ways, that Joe, Winnie, and he get along just fine. I don't know what else he can say, but I was hopin.'

I'm going mad over that platform test. I don't like the way I've written it, I haven't learned it yet, and I'm sure I'll make a darn fool of myself Saturday. Probably make a fool of Emily Dickinson, too.

I was in most of the day, had scenery class at 2:30, sat through it in my usual foggy state, and went over to Scott Hall with Jan, who's in my scenery class. Jan Hall, this is, not Frankel. We chatted away over Hostess cup cakes and coffee, then went on our separate ways, I, to the library, to look up editorial opinion on the way the Yalta conference settled Poland. By now I'm hopelessly confused on what happened in the Atlantic, Terehan, Bretton Oaks, Dumbarton Oaks, Crimea, here, there and everywhere. If anything did happen, which I doubt. I want to write a prospectus for a program which would read editorial opinion on a matter like Poland. I think it would be interesting, although very difficult to handle. I probably wouldn't listen to it, of course.

I wonder whether you get my mail. I wonder whether you will get this V-mail letter any faster than a regular one. I wonder where you are, what you're doing, how life is treating you.

> Suspense is hostiler than Death,
> Death, tho'soever broad,
> Is just Death, and cannot increase –
> Suspense does not conclude,
> But perishes to live anew,
> But just anew to die,
> Annihilation plated fresh
> With Immortality.
>
> _____
>
> You see, I cannot see your lifetime,
> I must guess,
> How many times it ache
> For me today—Confess
>
> How many times for my far sake
> The brave eyes film.
> But I guess guessing hurts,
> Mine get so dim!
>
> Too vague the face
> My own so patient covets,
> Too far the strength
> My timidness enfolds;
> Haunting the heart
> Like her transplanted faces,
> Teasing the want
> It only can suffice.
>
> —Emily Dickinson

I love you, dearest, SAD, sweetest—

Estelle

On March 5, I returned at 11:30 p.m. to the boarding house where I was living. No one seemed to be awake. The house was quiet, the light in the hall, low. On the hall table I found an envelope addressed in an unfamiliar handwriting, containing only a small newspaper clipping from the New York Times:

"First Lieut. Sidney Diamond who was with the Eighty-Second Chemical Battalion," the March 2 article reported, "was killed on Luzon." On January 29 he was killed by a Japanese knee mortar while acting as forward observer during an assault on Fort Stotsenburg, north of Manila. "Lieutenant Diamond, who served nineteen months in the South Pacific, received two citations…

Lieutenant Diamond was studying chemical engineering at City College when he entered the Army. Besides his parents he leaves a sister, Mrs. Anita Diamond Nicholson."

AFTERWORD

Although I suspect it was Sid's mother who sent me the obituary, I never found out for certain.

Outwardly my life seemed to change very little after I learned on March 5 of Sid's death, but I felt the despair of living without hope.

I resumed classes after a few days. Friends saw to it that I never had to eat a meal alone. But nights in the quiet of my spartan room at the boarding house were filled with questions about the past and the future. Just where and how had he been killed? Did he suffer? Was he sure of my love? These and myriad unanswerable questions tormented me. April 11 would have been Sid's twenty-third birthday. I wrote in my diary a passage from William Butler Yeats:

"O that so many pitchers of rough clay
Should prosper and the porcelain break in two!"

I thought about Sid's qualities of mind and heart which had made me fall in love with him when we were little more than children. He was a boy, and then a young man, who was impelled to act in accordance with his ideals, "not just talk about them." Although Sid had written that he would "not go off the deep end again" and that there were to be "no more crusades" for him, I wondered whether this would have been true. Despite the bitterness that mingled with my grief, I regretted every hurt I had inflicted with recriminations for his having left me to enlist. I regretted the fact that we had never consummated our love physically.

I was a spectator, emotionally numb, in the celebration of V-E day on May 8, Memorial Day, and V-J day on August 15, wishing only that Sid could know the war was over.

After being awarded the degree of master of arts "with distinction" and receiving an award for my direction of a play by Edna St.Vincent Millay, I returned home at the end of August for a short visit, and in September 1945 began my first teaching appointment, at the University of Alabama, teaching speech and theatre. At the end of that academic year, I returned to New York. In 1947 I was appointed to a teaching position at Queens College, in Flushing, New York, from which I retired in 1986.

I did fall in love again and have now been happily married for almost 40 years.

I cherish the memory of Sidney Diamond. He lives on in that alcove of the heart he asked me to reserve for him. I think often, with love and pain, of the young man who gave himself to fight in support of the country in whose principles he deeply believed.

It was not until January 2004 that I learned that Sid had been awarded the Silver Star "For gallantry in action at Luzon, Philippine Island, on 29 January 1945. When the mortar platoon which he commanded was committed to the support of an infantry battalion attacking well-prepared enemy positions, Lieutenant Diamond successfully directed mortar fire during the initial stages of the action, killing and wounding an estimated reinforced platoon of Japanese. In order to bring fire upon other enemy positions, Lieutenant Diamond, with heroic disregard for his own safety, voluntarily made his way alone under intense hostile machine gun, mortar and rifle fire to a position 150 yards beyond our lines. Despite continued heavy fire he remained in this position and skillfully directed his mortars in destroying many Japanese troops and strong-points until he was killed by an enemy shell. Lieutenant Diamond's indomitable courage, determination and skill were in keeping with the highest traditions of the military service."

We can only imagine what a man of his intelligence, character, and dedication might have contributed in a time of peace instead of war.

ABOUT THE AUTHOR

Estelle Spero Lynch was born and brought up in New York, graduated from Hunter College at the age of 19, Phi Beta Kappa, and after an interval working on war equipment at Bell Labs during World War II, earned the degree of master of arts in theatre and radio from Northwestern University. She taught speech and theatre at the University of Alabama, was a speech therapist, has been active in community theatre, and taught speech and English for over 30 years at Queens College. Her book for students of English as a Second Language, titled *Reading for Academic Success,* was published by Macmillan.

She lives in New York with her husband.

CPSIA information can be obtained
at www.ICGtesting.com
Printed in the USA
BVHW040627101222
653920BV00005B/83